THE COMPLETE GUIDE TO MOVIES
BEHIND THE SCENES

![Sandy Creek New York logo]

An Imprint of Sterling Publishing Co., Inc.
1166 Avenue of the Americas
New York, NY 10036

SANDY CREEK and the distinctive SANDY CREEK logo are registered trademarks of Barnes & Noble, Inc.

Text © 2016 by QEB Publishing, Inc.
Illustrations © 2016 by QEB Publishing, Inc.

All rights reserved. No part of this publication may be reproduced, stored in a retrieval system, or transmitted in any form or by any means (including electronic, mechanical, photocopying, recording, or otherwise) without prior written permission from the publisher.

ISBN 978-1-4351-6356-0

Manufactured in Guangdong, China
Lot #:
2 4 6 8 10 9 7 5 3 1
08/16

www.sterlingpublishing.com

Please note that some of the movies included in this book have not received a G, PG, or PG-13 rating.

THE COMPLETE GUIDE TO
MOVIES
BEHIND THE SCENES

CAROLINE ROWLANDS

CONTENTS

ALL ABOUT MOVIES 6
IN THE BEGINNING 8
SHOW BUSINESS 10
GLOBAL INDUSTRY 12
STAR POWER 14
HOW TO MAKE A MOVIE...PART 1 16
HOW TO MAKE A MOVIE...PART 2 18
CINEMATIC TECHNIQUES 20
TECHNOLOGY WONDERS 22
MOVIE GENRES 24
MOVIE STUDIOS THEN 26
MOVIE STUDIOS NOW 28
DEVELOPMENT 30
MONEY, MONEY, MONEY! 32
SCREENPLAY RULES 34
TELLING A STORY 36
MAKING IT HAPPEN 38
GETTING IT OUT THERE 40
PRE-PRODUCTION 42
PRODUCTION DESIGN 44
STORYBOARDS 46
CASTING 48
THE CREW 50
TEAMWORK 52
LIGHTS, CAMERA, ACTION! 54
LOCATION, LOCATION, LOCATION! ... 56
SETTING THE SCENE 58
MOVIE COSTUMES 60
MAKE-UP 62
HAIR-RAISING EFFECTS 64
PERFECT PROPS 66
SETTING THE SCHEDULE 68
READY TO ROLL 70

ON SET	72
ACTION!	74
SOUNDSTAGE	76
MOVIE MAGIC	78
CAMERA CONTROLLER	80
LIGHTING EXPERTS	82
MOVIE SOUNDS	84
GREEN SCREEN	86
DIGITAL PERFORMERS	88
SUPER STUNTS	90
STUNT PERFORMERS	92
POST-PRODUCTION	94
EDITING SUITE	96
EARLY VISUAL EFFECTS	98
VISUAL EFFECTS TODAY	100
CGI	102
AMAZING ANIMATORS	104
ANIMATION STUDIOS	106
AMAZING AUDIO	108
SOUND SOLUTIONS	110
MUSIC MASTERPIECES	112
TITLE SEQUENCES	114
CLOSING CREDITS	116
DISTRIBUTION	118
BUILDING THE HYPE	120
THE ROAD TO SUCCESS	122
MOVIE RELEASE	124
MOVIE THEATERS	126
FAMOUS THEATERS	128
HOME MOVIES	130
AWARDS SEASON	132
FESTIVAL FUN	134
MAKE YOUR OWN MOVIE	136
GLOSSARY	138
INDEX	142

ALL ABOUT MOVIES

If you've always wondered how a movie is made and want to find out more about all the different skills and processes involved in creating a motion picture, then this is the book for you! Read on to discover everything there is to know about how a movie is created plus facts and stats on all your favorite movies.

The original *King Kong* (1933) was a monster hit.

Working in the movies

Learn all about the different kinds of jobs that exist in the movie industry. From **cinematographers** and **producers**, to **gaffers** and **best boys**, this book explains who does what. You'll also learn about the pre- and **post-production** work that is needed to create a movie and distribute it to a worldwide audience.

MOVIE FACT

Since 1900, there have been around 2,500 movies made each year, around the world.

King Kong was remade in 1976, using a mechanical gorilla around 40 feet tall.

The 2005 *King Kong* used motion-capture technology.

History of movies

This book also takes you on a **behind-the-scenes** journey through the history of movie making, from the first cameras and motion pictures of the early 1800s and the people who invented them, to the amazing digital **CGI** (computer-generated imagery) **blockbusters** of today. The three movie versions of *King Kong* are a great example of the ever-changing technology used to create movies and how new innovations affect how movies are made.

IN THE BEGINNING...

People have been making movies to entertain audiences around the world for over 100 years. Read on to discover how motion pictures have evolved from short, black-and-white productions to the slick, hi-tech features we see on the big screen today.

Incredible inventors

It was the collaboration of several great inventors that brought the first moving pictures to life in the 1800s. George Eastman's roll film, Thomas Edison's Kinetoscope, and the Lumière brothers' Cinematograph were some of the early instruments of movie making and the start of a technology that changed the world.

The Lumière brothers took their Cinematograph all over the world.

MOVIE FACT

During his lifetime Thomas Edison held more than 1,000 patents for his amazing inventions.

Movie magic

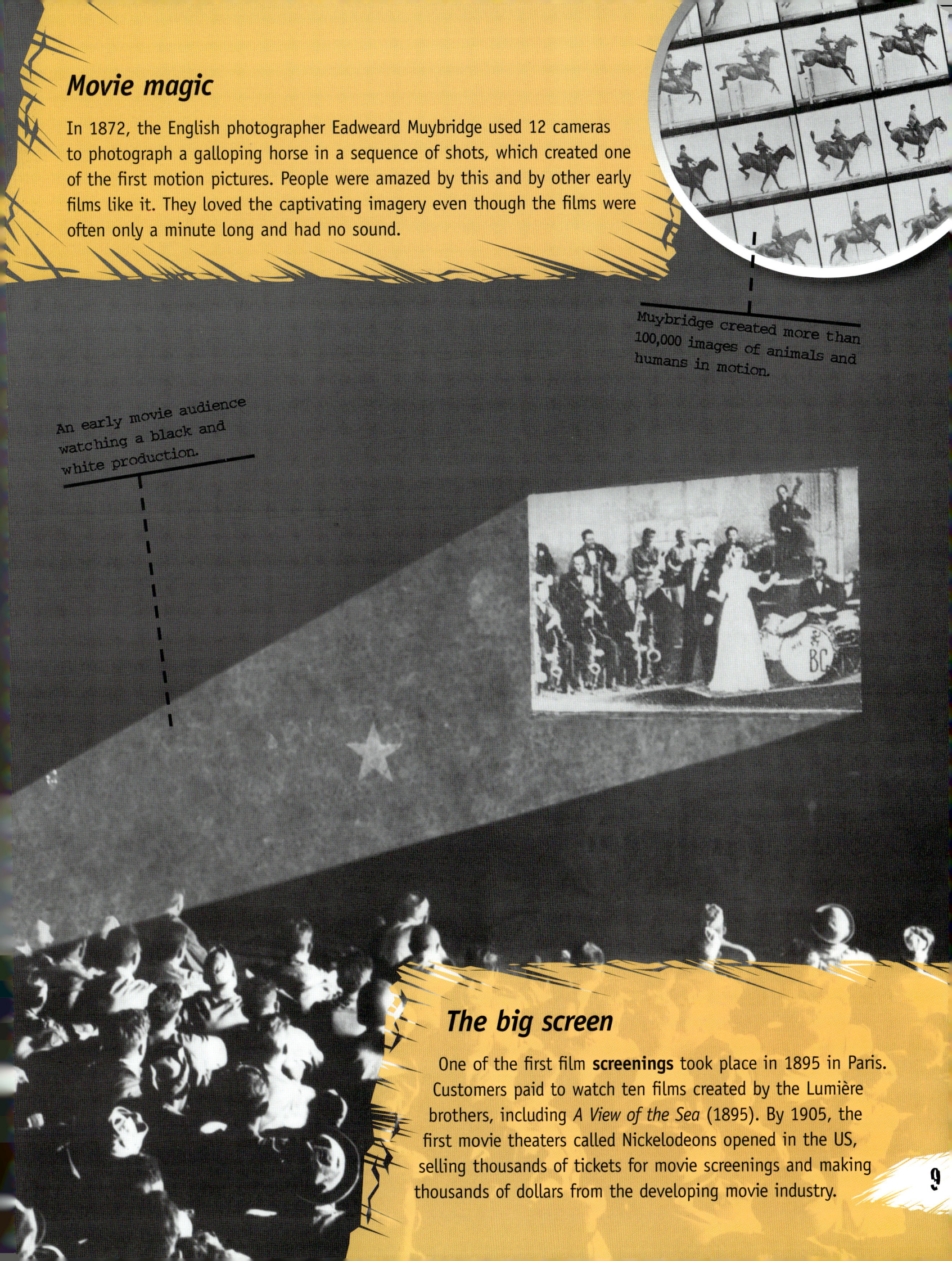

In 1872, the English photographer Eadweard Muybridge used 12 cameras to photograph a galloping horse in a sequence of shots, which created one of the first motion pictures. People were amazed by this and by other early films like it. They loved the captivating imagery even though the films were often only a minute long and had no sound.

Muybridge created more than 100,000 images of animals and humans in motion.

An early movie audience watching a black and white production.

The big screen

One of the first film **screenings** took place in 1895 in Paris. Customers paid to watch ten films created by the Lumière brothers, including *A View of the Sea* (1895). By 1905, the first movie theaters called Nickelodeons opened in the US, selling thousands of tickets for movie screenings and making thousands of dollars from the developing movie industry.

SHOW BUSINESS

As more movies were created and more money made, the movie industry began to grow. Amazing new filming techniques were developed, huge studios were built, and new movie stars were created.

Hooray for Hollywood

In the early 1900s, many movie companies moved from the east to the west coast of the US to avoid being fined by Thomas Edison's Motion Picture Patents Company, which owned all the patents for movie-making equipment. The Nestor was the first **studio** to open in Hollywood, California, in 1911. Paramount Pictures opened in 1912 and in 1918 four Polish brothers set up Warner Bros. on Sunset Boulevard in Hollywood.

Stars of the show

As Hollywood grew, so too did the roles of **directors** and **actors**. Directors began to receive recognition for the different techniques and technology they brought to their movies. The director DW Griffith pioneered new filming techniques, like his popular close-up shot, and the public began to idolize the famous actors they saw up on the big screen.

DW Griffith was so famous he was put on a 10 cent stamp.

Sound sensation

Movie makers began experimenting with sound in the early 1900s and *The Jazz Singer* (1927) was the first major movie presented as a "Talkie." It was a huge hit, but talking movies were treated more suspiciously elsewhere in the world, where movie makers worried that sound would spoil the creative and artistic elements of their motion pictures.

By 1929, Hollywood was making mostly "Talkies."

MOVIE FACT

One of the greatest Hollywood movie studios was never actually there. MGM was in Culver City, about 7 miles outside of Hollywood!

The original Hollywood sign was created in 1923.

Rainbow bright

The first color movies were made by the pioneer Edward Turner from England, who patented his color process in 1899. George Albert Smith patented his Kinemacolor system in 1906, but the later Technicolor technology (patented in 1926) was the most commonly used in Hollywood, as in *The Wizard of Oz* (1939).

It took a week to decide the exact shade of yellow for the yellow-brick road.

ii

GLOBAL INDUSTRY

While Hollywood is one of the oldest homes of movie making, movie studios and industries now exist all over the world. Lots of countries create their own style of movies and provide foreign and exotic locations for movies to be shot in.

The Mummy was shot at Atlas Studios in 1999.

Sony

With around a 17% share of the US and Canadian markets, Sony is considered one the biggest movie studios and owns lots of smaller movie companies such as Tri Star Pictures and Sony Pictures Animation.

Sandy studio

Atlas is the world's largest movie studio in terms of acreage, and it is located in the sandy Moroccan desert in Africa. Several of the *Star Wars* films were shot here and its giant Egyptian statues and tombs make the perfect **backdrop** for action-adventure movies.

Continental cinema

Cinecitta in Italy is the largest movie studio in Europe and where movie classics *Ben Hur* (1959) and *La Dolce Vita* (1960) were made. The more modern La Cité du Cinéma, in France, used to be a power plant but was transformed by the French director Luc Besson and opened for business in 2012.

Today, many movie, TV, and music productions are shot at Cinecitta.

MOVIE FACT

Studio Ghibli is a world-famous **animation** studio in Tokyo, Japan. Its leading movie maker, Miyazaki, never works with a script, preferring his ideas to flow.

Bollywood movies are often musicals.

Bollywood

Bollywood is the term used to describe the Mumbai-based movie industry in India. It is one of the biggest in the world and most of its movies are filmed at Film City, which produces more than 100 movies a year. Bollywood movies have inspired many western movies, including *Slumdog Millionaire* (2008) and *Moulin Rouge* (2001).

13

STAR POWER

There are all kinds of things that define a movie star's value, from how much money their movies make, to the number of awards on their mantelpiece, or how many people are following them on Twitter. Read on to discover some of the biggest and the best!

Franchises, like the Marvel movies, often make the most money.

Rich list

1. Robert Downey Jr. reputedly earned a whopping $40 million for his role in *Captain America: Civil War* (2016).

2. Jackie Chan makes his millions from movies like *Dragon Blade* (2015) and his Chan-branded merchandise.

3. Thanks to the successful *Fast and Furious* **franchise**, Vin Diesel is speeding his way to a huge payday. *Furious 7* (2015) took more than $1.5 billion at the box office.

Robert Downey Jr. writes and produces movies, as well as acts in them.

Most followed

1. @JLo (Jennifer Lopez) has more than 35 million Twitter fans thanks to her movie and music career.

2. @ActuallyNPH (Neil Patrick Harris) who starred in *The Smurfs* (2011) has 22 million followers.

3. @EmWatson's (Emma Watson) magical tweets have earned the star more than 21 million fans.

Emma tweets about movies and women's rights.

MOVIE FACT

Talent agencies get the best deals for their star clients and are often some of the most powerful people in the movie business. The big players are Creative Artists Agency, WME, and UTA.

Star performer

Katharine Hepburn holds the best actor record with her four Oscar wins! Hot on her heels are Meryl Streep and Jack Nicholson, with three each.

Jennifer Lawrence bagged her first Oscar at just 22 years of age, so she has plenty of time to catch up.

15

HOW TO MAKE A MOVIE... PART 1

Making a movie is not a simple process. It takes a lot of time, a lot of people, and a lot of hard work. The first stage of creating a movie is called **pre-production** and it includes all the processes needed to get everything ready to film the movie.

Steven Spielberg planning a shot for *Raiders of the Lost Ark* (1981).

Treatments and budgets

Every movie starts with a great idea, then a **treatment** is created. A treatment is the idea written as a story, but with loads of detail, from location to props and even sounds. From the treatment a **budget** can be created, including the costs of everything from the actors and **locations** to travel and even food expenses.

Teamwork

Finding the right people to work on a movie is a difficult job. A producer helps put together the team, from the director and actors, to the **costume designer** and sound engineers. Next comes the **script** or **screenplay**. This is given to the director and actors before filming starts so that everyone knows their lines and what they need to do for each scene. Sometimes a **storyboard** is also created, a kind of visual comic strip showing how the movie will look once created. An **animatic** is an animated storyboard, normally a slideshow, including examples of the **soundtrack** plus recorded sound effects and the cast's dialogue.

MOVIE FACT

The Wizard of Oz (1939) had a lot of production problems with more than 16 writers working on its script and 6 directors hired and fired to direct it.

A movie set being built.

Schedule of works

While actors are learning their lines, designers are creating the **sets**, **props,** and **costumes**, and technicians are preparing the necessary equipment. A shoot schedule is created ahead of **production**. It will help the director know what order to film in, when they will be filming, and what they will need for each shot.

HOW TO MAKE A MOVIE... PART 2

The next stages of making a movie are in production, which is when the actual filming takes place, and the post-production stage, when the shots filmed are edited and music, sound, and **special effects** added.

Filming

When filming begins, lots of different angles and distances are tried out to create lots of footage to work with in the editing studio. During filming, a movie's **press manager** will create lots of buzz about the movie, driving traffic to the movie's website and starting to engage with the movie's potential audience.

Steve McQueen filming on location for *12 Years a Slave* (2013).

Editing

Once shots are filmed, they are passed to the **editing** studio for editing. They are then cut or re-ordered until the movie is ready to show. **Automatic Dialogue Replacement** is when the actors are recorded redoing any dialogue that wasn't clear and sharp the first time around, when filmed on location. Music is added to scenes, which can either be existing songs or music specially created for the movie to create its soundtrack. Sound effects are created by **Foley artists**, who are people who record sounds like footsteps.

MOVIE FACT

Birth of a Nation (1915) was the first movie to have music specially composed for it.

Test screenings provide useful feedback and sometimes result in new scenes being added to or existing scenes deleted from the final cut.

Final cut

Cuts of the movie are shown to small audiences, **feedback** is taken, and editing continues on the movie until it's perfect. Once the editing is done, opening and closing titles are added, listing everyone involved with the movie. A final dialogue script is created if the movie is to be translated for different foreign territories, or **subtitled**. A good movie **trailer** is vital to help sell the movie. Once this is done, the movie can be marketed, sold, and then finally shown to the audience.

19

CINEMATIC TECHNIQUES

Cinematography is the art of visual storytelling. The artistry comes in controlling what the audience sees and doesn't see and how the image is presented. Read on to learn about some of the most popular techniques and understand your tracking shots from your Dutch tilts.

MOVIE FACT

The first rotating cameras, for taking panning shots, were built in the late 1890s.

A close-up in The Good, the Bad and the Ugly (1966).

Arc shot
A shot where the actor or location is circled by the camera.

Aerial shot
This shot is filmed from the air and often used to show an exciting location.

Bridging shot
A shot that demonstrates a shift in time or location.

Close up
This shot keeps only the full face in the frame.

Deep focus
A shot that keeps the foreground, middle ground, and background all in sharp focus.

Dolly zoom
The camera goes forward while at the same time zooms out, creating a very unsettling effect.

Dutch tilt
This is when the camera is tilted to create an odd angle.

A Dutch tilt in The Third Man (1949).

An establishing shot in *Skyfall* (2012).

Establishing shot
This shot often kicks off a scene, to establish where it is.

Handheld
A shot filmed with the camera in hand, to create a jerky feel.

High angle
A shot that looks down on a character, making them seem more vulnerable.

Locked-down
For this shot, the camera is fixed in one position, while the action continues elsewhere.

Long shot
A shot which shows an actor or character's entire body.

Low angle
This shot looks up at a character to make them look bigger and more imposing.

Medium shot
A common technique, showing more than a close-up but less than a long shot.

Money shot
The most expensive shot to shoot, but it has the WOW factor!

POV shot
This shot shows a scene from the point of view of one character, through their eyes.

Tracking shot
A shot that follows the character through the action.

A camera operator preparing for a high angle shot.

The money shot in *Independence Day* (1996).

TECHNOLOGY WONDERS

Movie makers have always been champions of the latest technologies. From the Lumière brothers' Cinematograph to **green screens**, the movie industry is an innovative one and, with increasing computer intelligence, it promises even more thrilling improvements to come.

Destination anywhere

Thanks to digital backgrounds, directors can let their imaginations run wild and actors can appear in exotic and make-believe destinations without having to leave the studio. *Sky Captain and the World of Tomorrow* (2004) was one of the first big-budget movies that was filmed completely with computer-generated backgrounds.

A new dimension

Set, costume, and prop creators design with CGI and **CAD** (computer-aided design) software. Turn to page 102 to discover more about CGI.

3D printers are used to create props and sets.

Home movies

Filmmakers are constantly creating new sensory experiences in the theater. This can lead to improvements to the personal home movie experience as well. Clever apps and amazing games, released alongside the movie, enable the audience to not just watch, but play and interact with the movie and the world it is set in too.

Screens are getting larger in homes and theaters.

Sky Captain and the World of Tomorrow (2004) took just 29 days to film.

MOVIE FACT

The cast of the 3D film Avatar (2009) wore leotard-like costumes covered in sensors that fed their movements back to computers that created the CGI imagery to create the movie.

Room with a view

An **IMAX** screen is gigantic, filling a viewer's field of vision to give them an incredible feeling of immersion, like they're moving through the movie while they watch it. Viewers can also wear special glasses to watch 3D movies, which are three-dimensional and enhance the perception of depth in a movie.

IMAX creates visually intense 3D movies.

23

MOVIE GENRES

Movies are defined by different genres. As directors and writers become more inventive in how they tell a story, and the technology becomes more advanced, the number of genres continues to grow. Describing a movie by its genre is an easy way of letting the audience know what to expect and, more importantly, if it's the kind of movie they're going to enjoy.

Packing a punch

The action and adventure genre grips the audience right from the start, with high-energy physical **stunts**, fast-moving sequences, and edgy dialogue. Usually set against a dramatic backdrop, the movie's hero bravely battles against an evil enemy and/or a life-threatening situation.

SUBGENRE The epic movie genre is one of the greats, with its main character usually trying to achieve a goal. Most end well, leaving viewers exhausted but satisfied.

SUBGENRE Disaster movies either focus on a global catastrophe, like the threat of deadly dinos in *Jurassic World* (2015), or on a group of people that need to be saved, like Jack and Rose in *Titanic* (1997).

Man versus dinosaur in *Jurassic World* (2015).

Ha, ha!

The comedy genre entertains through laughter. Whatever the plot, a comedy will exaggerate its narrative, characters, and dialogue to give viewers a couple of hours of pure escapism. This popular genre often showcases the talents of a specific actor or comedian.

James Marsden and Katherine Heigl in *27 Dresses* (2008).

SUBGENRE Rom-Com (Romantic Comedy) movies usually follows a successful set formula, blending a light-hearted plot with likeable characters, humor, romance, and a happy ending, as seen in *27 Dresses* (2008).

SUBGENRE Spoof films mock and impersonate other movie genres, taking the darkness of horror movies or gritty action of westerns and turning them into something side-splittingly hilarious.

Stick 'em up

The crime genre lends itself to all kinds of criminal capers, from your basic cops and robbers plot to the rise and fall of a criminal mastermind. Main characters can be the villains, the goodies out to capture them, or the legal brains that deliver justice.

Marlon Brando in *The Godfather* (1972).

SUBGENRE
Spine-chiller thrillers revolve around suspense, building the tension to ensure the audience is nibbling its nails, on the edge of its seats, right up to the twist at the end.

SUBGENRE
Gangster movies are usually moral tales, telling the rags-to-riches story of a central, often heroically portrayed character who has turned to a life of crime to survive, like *The Godfather* (1972).

MOVIE FACT
Box-office smashes often fuse different genres together, like the Star Wars saga, which uses the force of sci-fi, comedy, action, and adventure.

Outta this world

Taking escapism to a whole other level, fantasy movies transport viewers to a place that wouldn't exist in real life, telling a magical, mythical or futuristic tale. This genre also crosses over into horror films, which entertain by terrifying the viewer with eerie events and creepy characters.

SUBGENRE
Using the latest technology, a sci-fi film combines amazing special effects with visionary storytelling to transport its characters and the viewer into a futuristic parallel universe.

SUBGENRE
Animation movies transport viewers to make-believe worlds, like inside a girl's head in *Inside Out* (2015). Mostly aimed at kids, it's a genre secretly enjoyed by grown-ups too.

Pixar hit, *Inside Out* (2015).

MOVIE STUDIOS THEN...

A movie studio is an entertainment company that produces and sells movies. Hollywood has dominated the US and global movie-making industry for more than a century, building some of the biggest studios in the world that are still in business today.

Circus acts

Thomas Edison built the first movie studio in the US in 1893 and invited circus performers and dramatic actors to star in his motion pictures. He then distributed the movies to museums, theaters, and fairgrounds around the country and charged people to watch them.

Thomas Edison was born in Ohio in 1847.

The Big 5

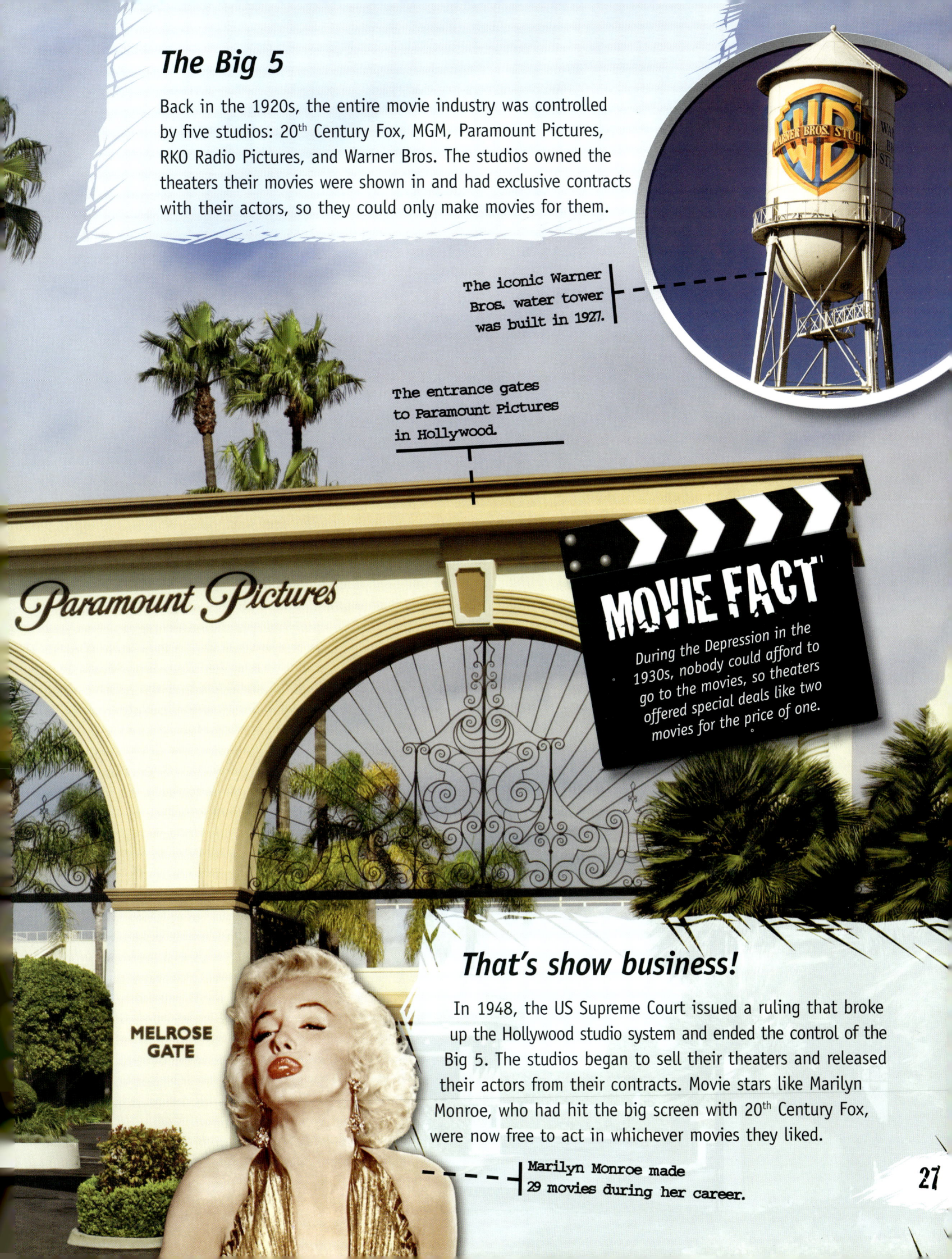

Back in the 1920s, the entire movie industry was controlled by five studios: 20th Century Fox, MGM, Paramount Pictures, RKO Radio Pictures, and Warner Bros. The studios owned the theaters their movies were shown in and had exclusive contracts with their actors, so they could only make movies for them.

The iconic Warner Bros. water tower was built in 1927.

The entrance gates to Paramount Pictures in Hollywood.

MOVIE FACT

During the Depression in the 1930s, nobody could afford to go to the movies, so theaters offered special deals like two movies for the price of one.

That's show business!

In 1948, the US Supreme Court issued a ruling that broke up the Hollywood studio system and ended the control of the Big 5. The studios began to sell their theaters and released their actors from their contracts. Movie stars like Marilyn Monroe, who had hit the big screen with 20th Century Fox, were now free to act in whichever movies they liked.

Marilyn Monroe made 29 movies during her career.

MOVIE STUDIOS NOW...

Today, there are several major US movie studios dominating Hollywood, including 20th Century Fox, Warner Bros., Pictures of Time Warner, Paramount Pictures, Walt Disney Pictures, Columbia Pictures, and Universal Pictures.

Warner Bros. backlot in Burbank, California.

MOVIE FACT

Tangled (2010) was the most expensive animation ever made, costing around $260 million. It took six years to make and lots of expensive computer coding to create Rapunzel's hair.

Warner Bros. studio has sets including a town center and a jungle.

Studio tour

These large movie studios are usually hidden away, often behind high walls that protect the workers and stars from the press and fans. Studios also have **soundstages**, which are huge soundproof hangar-like buildings, and **backlots**, like this street at Warner Bros., where outdoor scenes are filmed.

Big earners

Universal Pictures was the most successful studio in 2015, becoming the first studio to release three films, *Jurassic World*, *Furious 7*, and *Minions*, that each made more than one billion dollars at the box office. Disney's *Star Wars: The Force Awakens* (2015) made over two billion dollars, bringing it into third place behind *Titanic* (1997) and *Avatar* (2009) as one of the biggest-selling movies of all time.

The Walt Disney Company bought Lucasfilm in 2006.

Big spenders

Pirates of the Caribbean: On Stranger Tides (2011) was one of the most expensive movies ever made, costing a whopping $400 million to make. *Harry Potter and the Half-Blood Prince* (2009) also cost hundreds of millions to make, so when it came to filming *Harry Potter and the Deathly Hallows* (2011), Universal Pictures decided to split it into two films, getting two movies for the price of one and a bigger profit.

Pirates of the Caribbean: On Stranger Tides (2011) is the fourth movie in the series.

DEVELOPMENT

Movie **development** is when the decision to make a movie is made and all the elements needed to make that movie are put in place. From securing the story to raising the money, creating a movie is like fitting together a jigsaw puzzle—the perfect picture is made one piece at a time.

Storytime

A movie maker might have a story written or use a story from a book, a play, or even a video game like *Mario Bros*. Once the story is written, its **rights** are bought and secured so that the movie maker owns it and can use it for their movie.

In Ed Wood (1994) the title character struggles to pitch and develop his movies.

The Player (1992), starring Tim Robbins, is a movie all about the politics and intrigue involved in making a movie.

Money talks

Once the story is ready, the movie maker will create a **pitch** to present to investors looking to invest and make money from the movie. They will also pitch it to the directors and stars they would like to be involved. The bigger the star or more talented the director, the more chance the movie has of being sold into theaters once it's made.

MOVIE FACT

Many of the biggest-selling movies are aimed at children, often using stories from popular books, like Harry Potter, or superheroes, like Marvel's Avengers.

Production line

Once the movie has been **greenlit** (given the go-ahead) and the money has been raised to make it, a production company is found. This is a company that puts together the dream team for planning and creating the movie, from the people who build the movie sets, to those that light them up and film the action.

A camera controller getting ready to shoot.

MONEY, MONEY, MONEY!

It's no secret that sinking the Titanic or chasing dinosaurs around an island costs big bucks. The biggest box-office hits typically cost the most to make, but whose money makes the movie world go around and why do they spend it?

Money matters

Financing a movie is a risky business and studios tend to share the risk with other investors. These could be rich people choosing to invest to be a part of the glamor of Hollywood, or entrepreneurs looking to make money, or even companies who want to advertise their products in a movie. Etch A Sketch in *Toy Story* (1995) saw its sales rocket after its starring role alongside Woody and Buzz.

Etch A Sketch, Mr. Potato Head, and Slinkies became popular again after appearing in the *Toy Story* movies.

MOVIE FACT

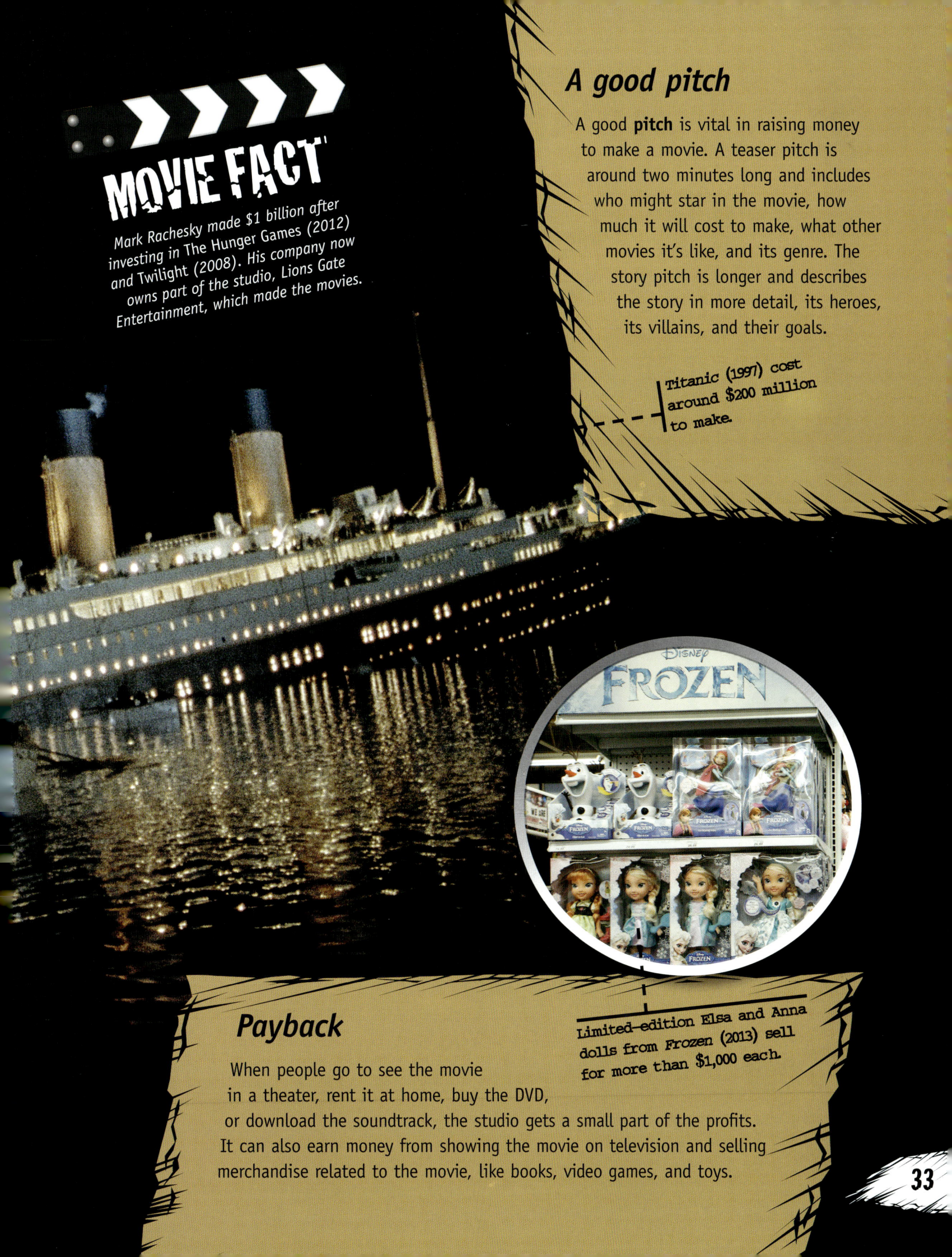

Mark Rachesky made $1 billion after investing in The Hunger Games (2012) and Twilight (2008). His company now owns part of the studio, Lions Gate Entertainment, which made the movies.

A good pitch

A good **pitch** is vital in raising money to make a movie. A teaser pitch is around two minutes long and includes who might star in the movie, how much it will cost to make, what other movies it's like, and its genre. The story pitch is longer and describes the story in more detail, its heroes, its villains, and their goals.

Titanic (1997) cost around $200 million to make.

Payback

When people go to see the movie in a theater, rent it at home, buy the DVD, or download the soundtrack, the studio gets a small part of the profits. It can also earn money from showing the movie on television and selling merchandise related to the movie, like books, video games, and toys.

Limited-edition Elsa and Anna dolls from Frozen (2013) sell for more than $1,000 each.

33

SCREENPLAY RULES

Making a movie takes lots of different skills and talents, but first and most importantly, you need a good idea and story. Once you have the story, the next stage is to create a screenplay, which is like a script but with more detail and information.

Tom Hanks and Emma Thompson check the screenplay for *Saving Mr Banks* (2013).

More than words

A screenplay is a document that tells the production team everything they need to know to make the movie. It will include the characters' dialogue, plus a description of anything else that should be seen and heard, for example any actions, locations, and sound effects. It shouldn't include any camera directions or anything the audience won't see.

A bright idea

Screenplay writers have to learn to sum up their ideas into a **logline**, which is a short, snappy sentence. For example, a theme park has a power failure and its cloned dinosaurs run wild. Or, a young man turns into a superhero spider and saves the day.

Good screenwriters stick to short, snappy sentences, like "Hobbits hide from orcs."

David Koepp crafted the screenplays for Spider-Man (2002), Jurassic Park (1993), and Mission: Impossible (1996).

MOVIE FACT

Charlie Chaplin was one of the earliest screenwriters, and his comedy scripts were packed with slapstick humor, drama, and sadness. He also acted, directed, and wrote music.

Screen action

Action described in screenplays should only show what the audience will see on screen, not what might have caused it or what a character thinks about it.

TELLING A STORY

What makes a good story? Most screenplays stick to a set formula. Who is the hero, what do they need, who is their adversary, and how do they defeat them to succeed?

Shrek (2001) mixed new characters with fairytale favorites.

Heroes and villains

All movies have a hero. A screenplay shows what that hero wants, what they need, and what their flaws are. They also usually have an adversary who they struggle with to overcome those flaws. For example, Shrek feels insecure and wants to be alone. Then he meets Fiona and Donkey, realizes he needs love, and defeats Lord Farquaad to save the day.

3 is the magic number

Successful screenplays usually follow a three-act structure, which includes the set-up, the confrontation, and a resolution. A good screenplay will grip the audience right from the start.

The opening scenes of E.T. the Extra-Terrestrial (1982) set up the story but also get straight into the action of the alien landing.

Ben Affleck became the youngest winner of a Best Original Screenplay Oscar when he won jointly with his friend Matt Damon.

MOVIE FACT

Matt Damon began writing the script for Good Will Hunting (1997) as an assignment for a writing class he was taking at Harvard University, before joining up with Ben Affleck to finish it.

Learn a lesson

Screenplays create obstacles and conflict so the hero has to struggle to get what they want. All good movies end with a lesson learned, whether it is to look after the planet, be tolerant of others, or never to give up on your dreams.

37

MAKING IT HAPPEN

Just as you can't have a movie without a story, you can't get the movie made without a production company. Hollywood studios are the main powerhouses of production, but small independent ones exist too, often led by the stars or directors themselves.

Bad Robot Productions

Owned by the successful producer JJ Abrams, Bad Robot Productions produces big Hollywood blockbusters like *Star Trek* (2009) and *Mission: Impossible—Rogue Nation* (2015). This company proves it is possible to combine dazzling special effects with exciting storylines.

JJ Abrams has also created hit TV shows like *Lost*.

WETA

After bringing Gollum to life in *The Lord of the Rings* (2002) and creating amazing CGI characters in *Avatar* (2009) and *Alvin and the Chipmunks: The Road Chip* (2015), WETA Digital is top of any fantasy film-maker's wish list thanks to its spectacular special-effects department and the extraordinary vision of its owner Peter Jackson.

With the help of WETA Digital, Peter Jackson brought *The Hobbit* to the big screen.

Pixar has created family favorites like *Toy Story* (1995) and *Monsters, Inc.* (2001).

Pixar

Originally started as part of Lucasfilm, the Apple creator Steve Jobs bought Pixar before selling it to The Disney Company. Pixar puts passion into every project and its success continues with its underwater adventure, *Finding Dory* (2016).

MOVIE FACT

Pixar's first animated short, *The Adventures of André and Wally B.*, was produced in 1984.

GETTING IT OUT THERE

Selling a movie and getting it seen by an audience obviously happens after the movie is created, but to ensure its success, it is important to set up the movie's **distributor** before filming starts.

In the 1930s, more than 65% of Americans went weekly to see a movie; today it's around 10%.

Deal makers

The most common kinds of distribution deals are split deals, where a movie distributor will decide where they want to sell a movie and how they want to sell it. They could only be interested in TV or DVD sales and leave other rights, like the toys and books, to a different company to buy.

The big screen

Getting a movie shown in theaters guarantees it attention in the media, be it in newspapers, magazines, or on social media. This helps let the public know it's coming, builds anticipation, and increases its value when it is released in other formats like online streaming or DVD.

20th Century Fox created a special social media campaign for the DVD release of The Wolverine (2013) which reached 15 million people.

MOVIE FACT

Some distributors spend more money on promoting a movie than they do on making it.

Slow payment

Getting paid for a movie can take a long time, sometimes years. Money from theaters around the world, DVD sales, and online or TV viewings takes a long time to reach the movie makers. In the 1940s, all profits from movies came from theater ticket sales, but today it is split between different viewing formats and merchandise.

PRE-PRODUCTION

Pre-production begins once a movie has been greenlit. All preparations for production are now set in motion and the key players, like director and actors, are put in place. On a small movie this can take a couple of months, but for bigger movies it can take more than a year to get everything ready to shoot.

People power

You can't make a movie without people and most movies involve an army of workers to create the costumes, props, and set designs, and to look after the actors once filming begins.

Most people who work on a movie set are freelance and are hired for the duration of the movie shoot.

MOVIE FACT

The Lego Movie (2014) took four years to make thanks to several rewrites of the screenplay and having to animate a lot of Lego bricks. It was all worth it though as everything in the movie is AWESOME!

Big budgets

At this stage, the production company should have a good idea of how much it will cost to make and distribute the movie. These costs will also help the company predict how much money the movie is likely to make.

Team effort

Everyone on the movie now gets to work, scouting locations, storyboarding the screenplay, creating schedules, and working together to have everything ready to go for the first day of filming.

Special vehicles, props and equipment have to be sourced too, like Ecto-1 in the original Ghostbusters movie. (1984)

43

PRODUCTION DESIGN

Production design is the art of storytelling through film. The look and style of a movie is created by the production designer, who is responsible for bringing the director's vision for a script or screenplay to life.

This painting appeared in the title sequence of *Gone with the Wind* (1939).

Production pioneers

Early films didn't have a production designer, but in 1939 David O. Selznick gave the job title to William Cameron Menzies, in recognition of his creative work on *Gone with the Wind* (1939). His vision for each set and how scenes would be filmed created a brilliant blueprint and a masterpiece of a movie that bagged 10 Oscars.

The Millennium Falcon was built from scrap metal sourced from airfields in England.

Crafty creators

A team of artists work to create sketches, models, storyboards, and photographs to help plan and film every shot and scene in detail. For the filming of the *Harry Potter* movies, a model of Hogwarts Castle was just one of the many projects for the movie's art department. When all the time spent on it was added up, it took 74 years to make.

In total, 86 artists worked on the Hogwarts model.

MOVIE FACT

Roger Christian's lightsaber creation in *Star Wars* (1977) was inspired by King Arthur's sword, Excalibur. Its glowing blades were created in post-production by a technique called rotoscoping.

Building dreams

Before the days of digital backgrounds, production designers had to create sci-fi worlds from scratch. Roger Christian worked on the very first *Star Wars* (1977) film and had to train his prop men to break up jet engines into scrap, then stick them back together to create the legendary Millennium Falcon.

STORYBOARDS

Storyboarding is the process of translating a screenplay into visual shots. For each shot there are several things to consider: from where the shot will be, who will be in the shot, what angle will the shot be filmed from, and what props or special effects are needed.

Walt Disney storyboarding with his animation team.

Disney idea

The storyboarding process was developed at Walt Disney Productions in the 1930s, evolving from comic-book sketches for how a scene would look and be shot. Within a decade, all of the animation studios were using storyboards, quickly followed by the live-action movie makers too.

Arrows are used to show movement on storyboards.

Comic creations

A storyboard is like a comic strip with a series of drawings detailing the sequence of events in a film. Sometimes labels are included, to show where actors will stand.

MOVIE FACT

The Lion King (1994) was the first Disney animated film to feature a completely original storyline and not one that was an adaptation of a preexisting story.

Shot list

Once movie makers have decided on what needs to be in their shots, they finalize their shot list and decide if they need to storyboard every shot or just the special ones. Sometimes shots are added in at this point too.

CASTING

Finding the perfect person to play a movie role is the tough job of a **casting director**. They have to find an actor the producer and director will want—someone who can act well, looks like the character, and, most importantly, whom the audience will like and believe in.

MOVIE FACT

Fashion and beauty vlogger Zoella was an extra in Harry Potter and the Philosopher's Stone (2001), but her scene in Professor Snape's potions class was cut.

Fishing for talent

A casting director will begin the search by contacting acting agencies with a brief telling the **agents** what they are looking for. Agents send video reels of their best talent, and the casting director selects a number of actors to audition.

Chloë Grace Moretz auditioned for the role of Katniss before Jennifer Lawrence got it.

Word perfect

Actors have to **audition** for the role in front of the casting director and often the producer and director too. They are asked to read a scene from the script and are given directions to act it in different ways. If they have a good audition, they're asked for a callback, where they'll audition again, this time with other actors who have already been cast, to make sure they work well together.

A casting call for the movie *Real Steel* (2011).

Team decision

The director, producer, and casting director will all have a say on which actors are chosen for the movie. Sometimes they choose on acting skill alone, but other factors are often taken into consideration too, from whether an actor is available to if they are the kind of actor their audience will like.

Extras!

A background actor, or **extra**, is a person who appears in a film in a non-speaking role. To be an extra you usually have to sign up with an agency, which provides background actors to production companies.

The film *Gandhi* (1982) used the most movie extras ever—a huge crowd of more than 300,000 people.

THE CREW

Do you ever watch a movie's **credits** roll by at the end of the film and wonder who all the people are? A movie crew can be made up of hundreds or even thousands of people. Read on to discover who's who on a set and what they do.

MOVIE FACT
Some producers direct, and some directors write and act too, like Tom Hanks, who directed, wrote, and starred in That Thing You Do (1996).

The boss

An **executive producer** sets up the finance of a movie but isn't involved in the day-to-day running of it. They hire a producer who runs everything for them. Some actors become producers too so that they can have more control over the movies they star in.

Kristen Wiig co-produced and acted in Bridesmaids (2011).

The vision

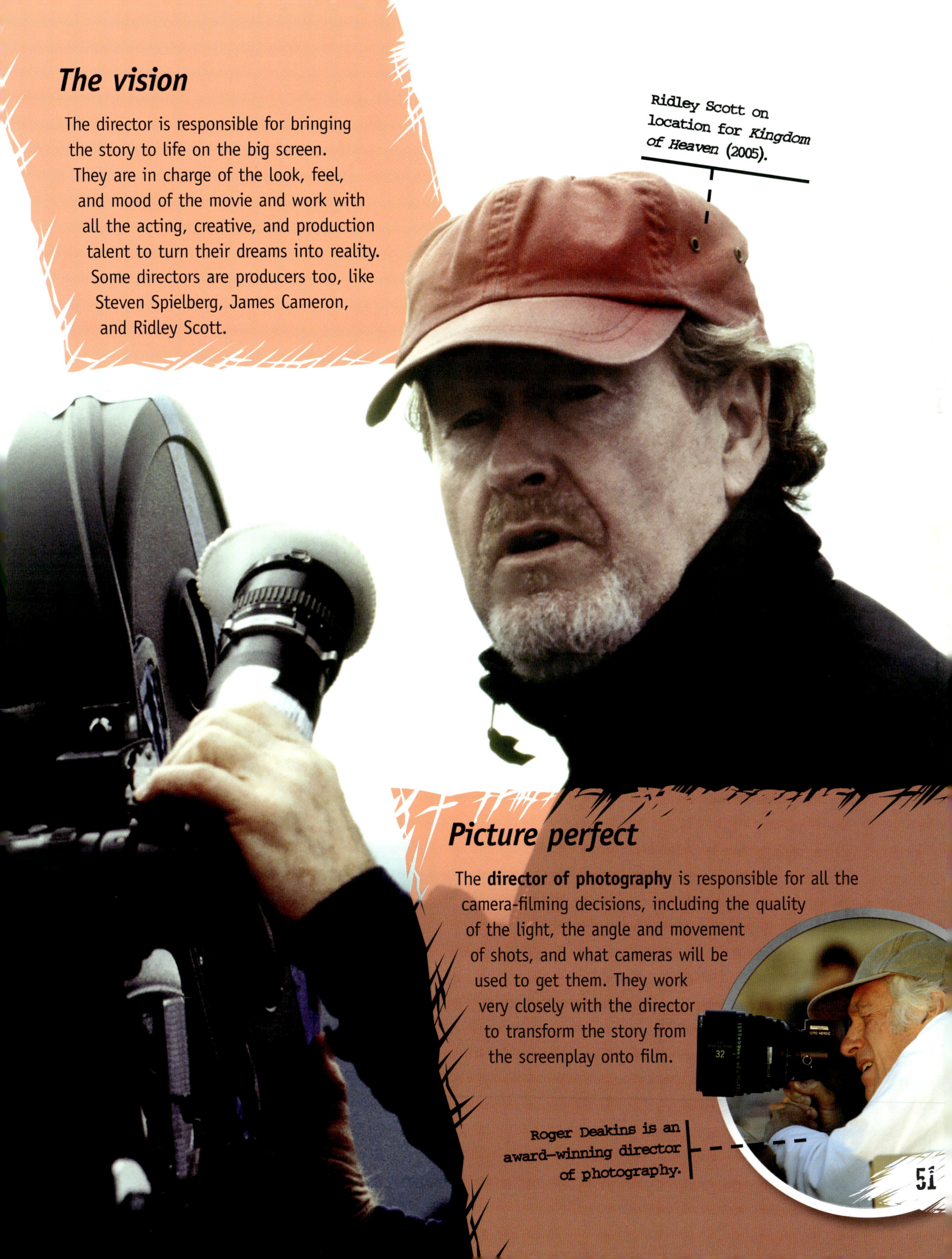

The director is responsible for bringing the story to life on the big screen. They are in charge of the look, feel, and mood of the movie and work with all the acting, creative, and production talent to turn their dreams into reality. Some directors are producers too, like Steven Spielberg, James Cameron, and Ridley Scott.

Ridley Scott on location for *Kingdom of Heaven* (2005).

Picture perfect

The **director of photography** is responsible for all the camera-filming decisions, including the quality of the light, the angle and movement of shots, and what cameras will be used to get them. They work very closely with the director to transform the story from the screenplay onto film.

Roger Deakins is an award-winning director of photography.

TEAMWORK

Under the big movie bosses are another army of workers, all working away to ensure the movie production process runs smoothly to help the director, producer, and director of photography get the shots they want.

The clapperboard (or slate) notes which scene is being shot and the number of takes.

Artists at work

The **art director** works with a team of artists, including the production designer, **set designer**, **prop master,** and many others to help realize the director's vision for the film. Whether it's painting a set, modeling props, or building entire fake cities, they're responsible for the look and feel of the movie.

The amazing characters in *Pan's Labyrinth* (2006) were mostly created with make-up and animatronics.

Helping hand

The role of **assistant director** is to help the director. Responsibilities include managing the shooting schedule, making sure everyone knows what they should be doing, and organizing the actors to be in the right place at the right time.

A film crew on a location shoot.

Movie manager

The **unit production manager** oversees the entire movie production including its paperwork, budgets, and schedules. The role is an important one and vital to ensure that everything runs smoothly, stays on schedule, and doesn't cost more money than it should.

ROLL

MOVIE FACT
The box office smash Iron Man 3 (2013) credits more than 3,000 crew members.

LIGHTS, CAMERA, ACTION!

On set, another band of movie makers get to work, ensuring everything is ready to go for when filming starts. While they don't have the same responsibilities of the bigger movie bosses, their roles are essential to ensuring the production's success.

MOVIE FACT
A best boy refers to the first assistant of a gaffer or a grip. If a woman is doing the job, she is known as a best girl.

Leading lights

A gaffer and **grip** help the director of photography on set. A gaffer is responsible for using the correct lighting equipment and filters to make sure all the lights are the right color and brightness. A grip builds and looks after all the rigging that supports the lighting and camera equipment.

Power players

The electrical team, led by a head electrician, are responsible for handling the power on a set. They make sure there is enough power to supply all the equipment and that the set is safe for all the other crew members and actors to work with.

Preparing to shoot a scene on the set of *2001: A Space Odyssey* (1968).

Able assistant

Depending on the size and budget of a movie, a production assistant's role can vary, but they are mostly responsible for acquiring equipment, making sure everyone has the right script and schedule, and arranging travel arrangements for the cast and crew.

On smaller shoots the production assistant even operates the clapperboard.

LOCATION, LOCATION, LOCATION!

Movies are made all over the world, in all kinds of exotic and exciting locations. Finding the perfect place to film a movie is the job of a **location scout** and an important part of creating movie memories an audience will never forget.

The mountainous terrain of New Zealand made a perfect Middle Earth in the Lord of the Rings trilogy.

MOVIE FACT

Nicholas Ray was a travel writer before he became a location scout and used his knowledge of Cambodia to find a picture-perfect setting for Lara Croft: Tomb Raider (2001).

Faking it

If a movie's location doesn't actually exist, a location scout does the next best thing and finds a spot that captures the feel of the setting in the screenplay. Locations all over New Zealand were used to shoot *The Lord of the Rings* and *The Hobbit* movies.

Popular movie locations

Central Park, New York, is the backdrop for many movies, including kids' classics *Home Alone* (1990), *The Smurfs* (2011), *Enchanted* (2007), *Elf* (2003), and *Night at the Museum* (2006). Ireland also features in many movies, but not always as itself. Scenes from the Scottish epic *Braveheart* (1995) were shot there, as well as the closing scene for *Star Wars: The Force Awakens* (2015). Niagara Falls provides the dramatic, and very wet, backdrop to box-office blockbusters *Superman II* (1980) and *Pirates of the Caribbean: At World's End* (2007).

Central Park in New York.

Star Wars: The Force Awakens' (2015) closing scenes were shot at Skellig Islands in Ireland.

Niagara Falls on the border of the U.S. and Canada.

SETTING THE SCENE

Set designers create the backdrop for a movie, conjuring up scenery that drives the storyline along as much as the action and dialogue. Sometimes a backdrop blends into the action, and other times its job is to transport the audience back in time or to a fantasy world.

Doodle design

A production or set designer usually begins with a rough drawing of how they imagine each set will look. Once the drawings are approved, the sets can be created. A set designer might use an existing building, or design and build something from scratch.

A production drawing of The Burrow, from The Hobbit series.

Surprise!

The set designers of *The Goonies* (1985) built a complete pirate ship for the movie.

The ship was hidden from the cast so that their surprise on seeing it for the first time could be caught on camera.

MOVIE FACT

Titanic's (1997) $200 million budget was more than the cost of the real ship itself.

The set designer on Titanic (1997) built a replica of the ship and two huge water tanks to sink it in!

MOVIE COSTUMES

Costumes are one of the many tools a director has to tell a story, and good costume designs are critical to a movie's success. Every piece of clothing worn in a movie is considered a costume, be it a scary, scaly alien suit or something simple, like a denim jacket. A designer's goal is for their costumes to blend and become a part of the story and help the audience understand the characters who wear them.

Telling a story

A costume designer works with the director and actors to support the narrative by creating realistic characters. After reading the script, the designer will research the period or world the film is set in, then consider the age of the characters and the scenes they will be acting in, to bring the director's vision to life.

MOVIE FACT
The talented Edith Head won a record-breaking 8 Oscars during her lifetime for her amazing costume designs.

Painting a picture

Every part of a costume, from the cut and shape of the clothes to their color and texture, helps create the scene's atmosphere and visually enhances the action. Designers also use color to show the personality of characters, which may go unnoticed by the audience, but will still affect how they think about them. In the case of iconic characters like Sherlock Holmes, a costume can help the audience connect with him before he has even uttered his first line.

The iconic deerstalker hat makes the audience feel they know the character.

Fashion experts have claimed the suit worn by Cary Grant in North by Northwest (1959) was the best suit in movie history and the most influential. Tom Cruise's character in Collateral (2004) and Ben Affleck's in Paycheck (2003) both wear suits that look just like it!

Trendsetter

Hollywood costumes influence fashion trends, and outfits worn in movies are quickly copied by designers. From Cher's over-the-knee socks in *Clueless* (1995), to Sandy's leathers in *Grease* (1978), fans follow the fashion and style, not just of the characters, but also of the star who plays them. The *Twilight* (2008) stars put a whole new spin on looking pale and mysterious and *The Hunger Games'* (2012) Katniss Everdeen's combats, parka, and braid created a signature look for Millennials all over the world.

Judianna Makovsky created the costumes for Katniss.

MAKE-UP

The make-up department on a movie set is responsible for the design, application, continuity, and care of make-up before and during filming. Not only do the actors have to look the part for the movie, but their make-up needs to last and look the same for every single shot.

Work of art

Nick Dudman was the creative genius behind the make-up effects, animatronics, and prosthetics for the *Harry Potter* movies. Voldemort's terrifying face took almost three hours to create each day.

Once made up, Ralph Fiennes, the actor who played Voldemort, was unable to eat!

MOVIE FACT

Nick Dudman's first make-up job was working on Yoda in The Empire Strikes Back (1980).

Artists at work

Most movie **make-up artists** have a qualification in a foundation make-up course, then train as an assistant. Key skills are creativity and artistic flair, and many have hairdressing talents too.

Make-up master

Greg Cannom is one of Hollywood's most versatile make-up artists. His creative skills have won two Oscars. One was for his transformation of Brad Pitt, from old to young, in The Curious Case of Benjamin Button (2008).

Greg Cannom transformed Robin Williams from male to female in Mrs. Doubtfire (1993).

63

HAIR-RAISING EFFECTS

From cutting and styling an actor's hair to researching wigs and hairpieces for fantasy or period movies, a **hairstylist**, like a make-up artist, must ensure each actor's look is true to character, looks good on camera, and is consistent at all times.

More than 20 hairstylists worked on *Marie Antoinette* (2006).

Makeover magic

The hairstyling team works with the make-up and costume departments to create a director's vision for a character. Whether it's making a performer look bald when they have lots of hair or creating realistic wigs and beards, magical styling creations transform actors from ordinary-looking people to the amazing characters seen on screen.

MOVIE FACT

Rick Baker has received the most Oscars for make-up and hair. He has won 8 in total, his first for An American Werewolf in London (1981).

Winning styles

In 1993, the Oscar award for Best Make-up was extended to include hairstyling too. Sometimes the hair is one of the most important parts of a character's look, like Kirsten Dunst's tresses in *Marie Antoinette* (2006), or can become an icon of the movie, like Audrey Hepburn's tiara and bun in *Breakfast at Tiffany's* (1961).

Hairstylist Nellie Manley created Audrey Hepburn's iconic bun.

Sometimes the working day began at 2am on *The Hunger Games* (2012) set.

Wig wonders

Ann Bray, who worked on *The Hunger Games: Catching Fire* (2013), began training her team of stylists before filming began. Up to 65 stylists worked on the movie and created more than 500 wigs, including the famous "rose" hairpiece worn by the character Effie Trinket.

PERFECT PROPS

The objects used in movies that enhance the scene and help tell the story are called props. Sometimes made specially, other times sourced from everyday life, the two main objectives of a prop are to look real to the audience but to be safe for the actor to use.

MOVIE FACT

In the movie Cast Away (2000), a prop volleyball is transformed with some paint to become a character called Wilson.

Weapons in movies are often made with safe materials, like foam.

Heroes and stunts

A **hero prop** is made with extra detail, as it will be seen in close-up shots or held by the lead actors. A stunt prop is something that looks exactly like it should, but is cleverly crafted so it won't hurt the actors when used.

Creative genius

A prop maker has to have imagination but also be practical. Specialist knowledge in computer design software and different materials, like polystyrene and foam, are vital, as is being able to operate machinery to make sets, furniture, and upholstery.

Problem-solving skills and creativity are a must for prop makers.

Dorothy's ruby slippers from The Wizard of Oz (1939) were snapped up for $660,000 at an auction in New York in 2000.

Movie memorabilia

Some fans love movies so much, they'll spend a fortune to get their hands on the most iconic props from them. In 2013, an auctioned Harry Potter elder wand sold for $10,000.

SETTING THE SCHEDULE

Once all the pre-production elements are in place and have been finalized, it's time to create the movie production schedule. The aim of the schedule is to make sure everything is filmed how the director wants it, on time, and within budget.

Perfect timing

The schedule is created by the director and assistant director. Trying to work out what scenes can be shot on the same day, where they'll be shot, and which actors and crew are needed to shoot them takes a lot of time and attention to detail.

The Lego Movie (2014) went off-schedule when the script was rewritten several times.

Lining the script

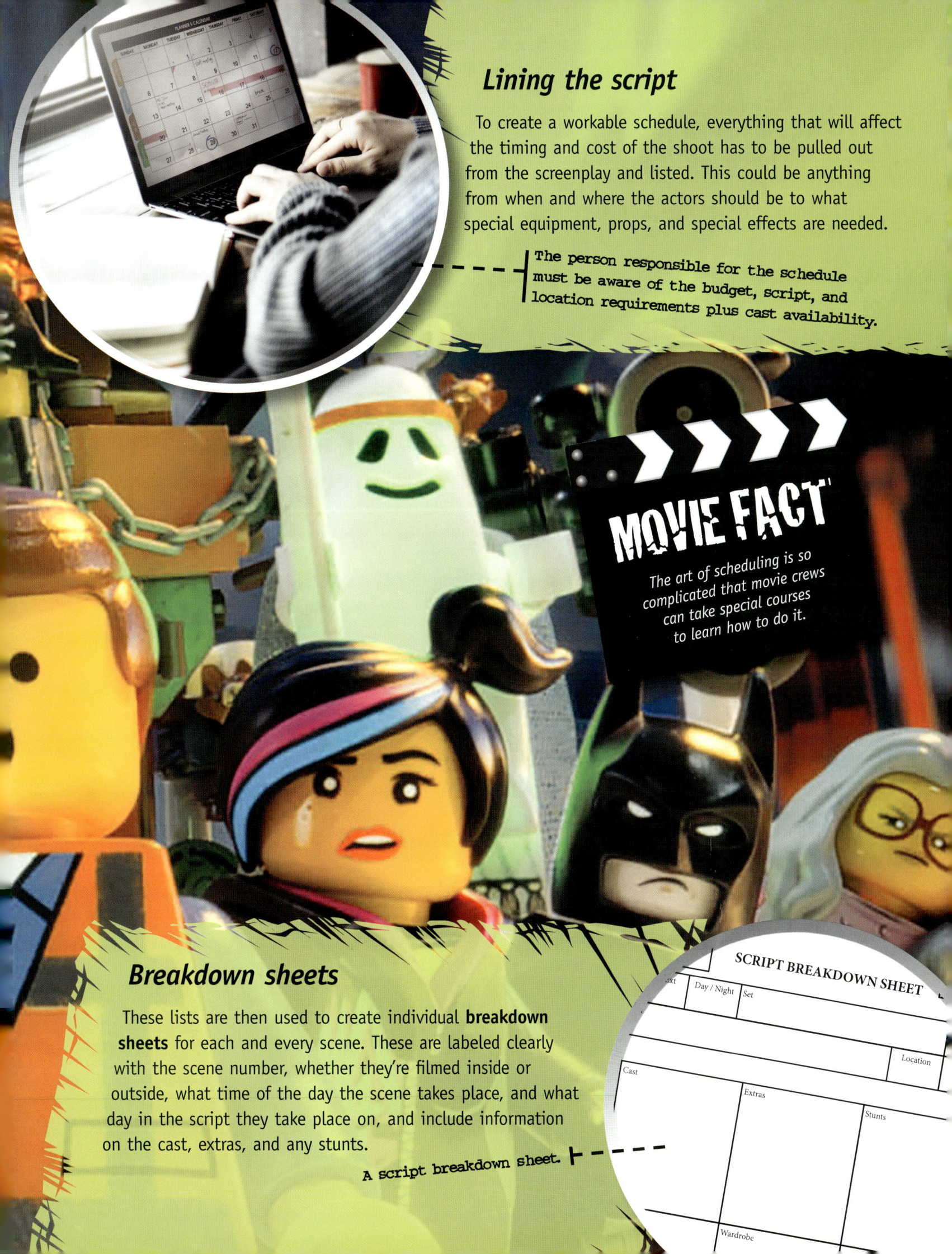

To create a workable schedule, everything that will affect the timing and cost of the shoot has to be pulled out from the screenplay and listed. This could be anything from when and where the actors should be to what special equipment, props, and special effects are needed.

The person responsible for the schedule must be aware of the budget, script, and location requirements plus cast availability.

MOVIE FACT
The art of scheduling is so complicated that movie crews can take special courses to learn how to do it.

Breakdown sheets

These lists are then used to create individual **breakdown sheets** for each and every scene. These are labeled clearly with the scene number, whether they're filmed inside or outside, what time of the day the scene takes place, and what day in the script they take place on, and include information on the cast, extras, and any stunts.

A script breakdown sheet.

READY TO ROLL

Once the production schedule is complete, the cameras can start rolling and the movie can be shot. The filming process on big-budget movies can be very complicated, involving many teams to create the look and the sound of the movie, from the actors themselves to the camera, sound, lighting, and digital technicians.

The cast and crew of *The Martian* (2015) were flown out to the red deserts of Wadi Rum in Jordan.

Traveling stars

If a film is shot on location, the entire cast and crew must be transported there. Sometimes they can be away from their families and homes for months at a time.

Practice makes perfect

During rehearsals, the various technicians can test out their camera, sound, and lighting equipment with the actors and director to ensure that when the cameras hit record, they get the shots they want and the scenes exactly how the want them.

The movement of the camera is as important as the movement of the characters, to get the right shot.

MOVIE FACT

The Red Bull Skydiving Team practiced for a week to create the scene where passengers fell from a plane in Iron Man 3 (2013).

Best shot

The director also experiments with how a scene or stunt might work. Sometimes scenes or stunts end up being shot entirely differently than how they were planned, especially if a stunt is considered too dangerous.

Stunt sequences can take months of planning to get right.

ON SET

A movie set is a place of work, just like any other business, and there are processes to follow, rules to keep, and goals to achieve. The working day starts early, with everyone expected to turn up on time and stay until the job is done.

MOVIE FACT

Steven Spielberg claims it took 50 takes to shoot one small scene in Jaws (1975), while Into the Woods (2014) director Rob Marshall always tries to get his shots in less than eight takes.

People work off and on camera, to get the perfect take.

Call sheets

Every actor and crew member receives a **call sheet** the night before filming. This tells them everything they need to know for the following day, from what time to be on set and where to be, to what facilities will be available.

Some call sheets even include a weather forecast.

Shooting steps

Each scene follows a step-by-step shooting process. Firstly, the director decides where the actors will be on the set, for the first camera position. This is called **blocking**. Then the technicians set the equipment for that shot, the shot is rehearsed, and the equipment is adjusted before the shot is finally filmed.

Most production teams use digital clapperboards today.

Take two

The iconic movie **clapperboard** is used to mark up scenes and takes during the movie's production. It's also used to help synchronize the picture and sound, as the sharp noise the clapperboard makes is easy to pick up on the audio track.

ACTION!

Principal photography is the term given to the actual filming of the movie. It is usually the most expensive phase of movie production and also the point of no return for movie financiers. Once a greenlit production gets to this stage, the movie usually goes on to be finished.

@DisneyStudios celebrated the end of its principal photography on *The Force Awakens* (2015) by revealing the movie's title to fans on Twitter on November 6, 2014.

Filming is a team effort.

Camera crew

A camera operator captures the action, under the direction of the director of photography. The first camera assistant (focus puller) is in charge of keeping the camera in focus. The second camera assistant operates the clapperboard (slate).

74

Dailies

At the end of each day, the shots from that day are synced to sound and reviewed by the director and other members of the crew. Known as dailies, they are checked for technical issues to ensure the actors were performing as they should and to check that all the right shots were captured.

MOVIE FACT

Some movies don't use dailies, as the movie footage is shown live on huge screens as it's recorded. This way, changes can be made as filming is happening.

Re-shoot

If a shot has gone wrong or been missed, the director will order a pick up or a re-shoot. Ideally these take place right away because, if they're not picked up till much later, the set may have been taken apart or the actors might be working on other projects.

Most big productions now build re-shoots into their schedules.

75

SOUNDSTAGE

A soundstage is a hangar-like soundproof building used to film movies and usually located on the property of a movie studio. There are thousands of soundstages around the world, used for movies, TV production, and concerts, too.

Currently Pinewood Studios in England has the biggest indoor soundstage, built in 1976 for *The Spy Who Loved Me* (1977).

Super size

Plans are in motion to turn the Superdome in Louisiana into the world's biggest soundstage, where up to 12 movies can be shot at the same time.

Golden oldie

One of the world's oldest soundstages is the old Warner Bros. studio, today called Sunset Bronson Studios. Built in 1919, this famous Hollywood site was where one of the first talking movie hits, *The Jazz Singer* (1927), was recorded. It is still in use today.

MOVIE FACT

The Oriental Movie Metropolis in China will house the world's first underwater soundstage.

Weather wonder

It may not be the biggest, but the G Star soundstage in Florida has its own weather system and can create forest fires, hurricanes, and rainstorms, all at the touch of a button. The studio is also available for a low fee if producers hire local high-school interns to work on their movies.

MOVIE MAGIC

Cinematography is the science or art of motion-picture photography, recording either digitally with an electronic image sensor or chemically with a light-sensitive material like film.

MOVIE FACT

The word cinema comes from the Greek word kinema-matos, meaning the science of pure motion.

Classic camera

Traditional movie cameras are mechanical and capture images on moving film. The film moves past the lens by either a wind-up mechanism or a small motor. Its shutter opens and closes to take a continuous series of photographs.

The series of photos combines to create a moving image.

Modern camera

Digital cameras use a grid of photo sensors to record the incoming pattern of light. Each sensor returns an electrical current when it's struck by the incoming light. The amount of current varies with the amount of light it captures, which the camera then uses to create an image.

Digital cameras save the film as data files.

The film crew on the set of To Catch a Thief (1955).

Popular choice

The Alexa by Arri, the Red Epic, and Cannon digital cameras are used the most in big-budget movies. Most movie makers now shoot digitally and are continuously experimenting with the equipment they use, to create different styles for their motion pictures (turn to page 20 for more on cinematic techniques).

79

CAMERA CONTROLLER

Cinematography is one of the most complex and challenging areas of movie making. A cinematographer is in charge of the camera and lighting crew on a movie set and often has the biggest teams to manage.

Almost the whole of *Gravity* (2013) was shot digitally with the Arri Alexa camera.

Be the best

Many cinematographers start their careers as photographers or camera operators. Understanding cinematography requires a lot of training that never ends. With technology constantly changing, cinematography is one of the most innovative and shifting art forms.

Pushing the boundaries

Emmanuel Lubezki is one of the most innovative cinematographers working today. He won an Oscar for his work on *Gravity* (2013) where he was faced with the difficult task of creating the right light and movement in space.

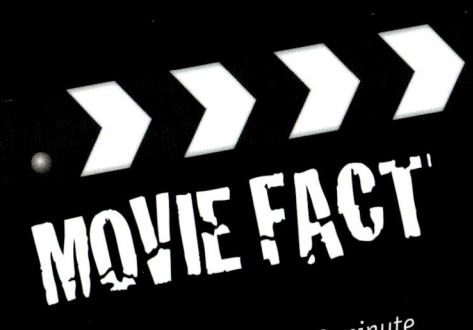

MOVIE FACT

Gravity's opening 12-minute scene took months to plan and years to shoot.

Sandra Bullock was strapped inside a lightbox for up to 10 hours a day during the filming of *Gravity*.

Scotland's weather was considered too unpredictable to create the right light, so *Brigadoon* (1954) was shot in MGM's studio instead.

Winning shots

Joseph Ruttenberg has the most Oscars for his cinematography work, with four awards for his movies including *Brigadoon* (1954) and *Gigi* (1958). Charles Lang was the youngest cinematography winner, bagging a gold statue for his camera vision when he was just 30 years old, for the movie *A Farewell to Arms* (1932).

LIGHTING EXPERTS

Understanding how lighting can change the feel and look of a movie is vital not just in a studio, but also on location. A good lighting technician can take a script and translate its meaning onto film with the use of light and, just as importantly, shade.

Basic lighting

Three-point lighting is one of the simplest ways of lighting a scene. It consists of a key light as the main source on the actor, a fill light opposite the key light to reduce any shadows, and a rim light.

A rim light, behind the actor, is used to separate them from the background.

Great gaffer

John Higgins, one of Hollywood's most successful lighting experts (gaffers), claims the biggest challenge is lighting large spaces in real-life locations.

In *The Bourne Ultimatum* (2007) John Higgins ingeniously lit up Waterloo Station in London using its natural light.

MOVIE FACT

Thomas Edison's Black Maria studio, built in 1892, was a rotating structure that allowed its glass roof to be positioned to follow the direct sunlight.

Movie moods

Creating the right mood for lighting relies on key, contrast, and tone.

1. The key is the relation between the amount of dark and light in a shot. High-key lighting is bright and cheery; low-key lighting is used to provide suspense and drama.

2. A lack of contrast between black and white in an image creates a dreamy, misty feel to a scene, while a high contrast between black and white creates tension and added drama.

3. Color can also affect how a viewer reacts to a movie. Warm colors like pinks and yellows make the audience feel comfortable and happy, while blues and darker tones can make the viewer feel serious.

The colors red and black are often used to signal danger and unsettle an audience, as in *Dracula* (1958).

MOVIE SOUNDS

A movie soundtrack is as complicated to create as the image itself. It is made up of sound effects, the human voice, and music. These three elements are synchronized with the imagery to create a multi-sensory experience for the audience.

Sound chain

Recording sound is a series of links in a chain. The sound itself is picked up by a microphone, then the cables and connectors carry the sound to the recording device, and the recording device then monitors the sound and captures it.

The microphone is always just out of shot, as seen here in the filming of *The Avengers* (2012).

The sound crew

A production sound crew often includes a **sound assistant,** who sets up and checks all the equipment before recording, **a boom operator**, who positions all the microphones to pick up the sound, and a **production sound mixer**, who is off set to record and capture the sound.

MOVIE FACT

Jurassic Park (1993) also won an Oscar for Best Visual Effects.

Gary Rydstrom won 2 Oscars in 1994 for his sound work on Jurassic Park (1993).

Amazing sounds

One of the hardest jobs for a sound technician is producing sounds that don't exist. *Jurassic Park's* (1993) T. rex roar was a mash-up of the roars of an elephant, an alligator, and a lion, a whale's breathing, and the grunting of a koala.

GREEN SCREEN

Historically, movie makers used paintings, models, and trick photography to create impossible-looking effects. Then along came green screens and **Chroma Key**, which changed the way movies were made forever.

Most of the fighting scenes were shot against green screens in The Matrix (1999).

How the same scene from The Matrix (1999) looked with the digital background in place.

How it works

Chroma Keying is a way of layering two image streams together. Scenes shot in front of a green screen enable actors to be separated from their background. Computer software checks the colors in the film and if it matches the Chroma Key color (green), it replaces that part of the film with a different background.

Magical moment

The green screen (originally blue when created) first appeared in Hollywood back in the 1930s. RKO Radio Pictures used it to create a magical genie in a bottle in *The Thief of Bagdad* (1940).

The Thief of Bagdad (1940) won an Oscar for its visual effects.

MOVIE FACT

Blue screens worked better with traditional film cameras (1940), but image sensors in digital cameras are more sensitive to green, making it the most popular color choice today.

Shadowy figures

Lighting is just as important when shooting against a green screen as any other backdrop. If a shadow is created, it might be seen as a darker color and not replaced by the digital background, which will then spoil a scene.

87

DIGITAL PERFORMERS

In the past, directors had to direct real actors against the green screen and then splice the actors and backgrounds together into one digital scene. The latest technology has developed ways to computer generate all aspects of a scene, from the backgrounds and landscapes to the actors themselves.

Motion magic

Bay Raitt and his animation team used motion, captured from Andy Serkis' expressive face, and traditional animation to create the character of Gollum in the *Lord of the Rings* movies. Andy Serkis also acted the part of Gollum on set, but was then digitally removed and replaced with the animated model.

Andy Serkis is considered one of the best actors for motion capture. He has won many awards.

Seeing double

The cutting-edge tools of **facial mapping** were used in *The Social Network* (2010) to let Armie Hammer play the two roles of the Winklevoss twins.

During post-production, some scenes required Armie Hammer's face to be digitally grafted over his body double's.

The character of Gollum took four years to create.

Super stunts

Fake or computer-generated actors are able to do anything, from flying around skyscrapers to dodging bullets, in both fast and slow motion. Actors can also now be digitally altered, aged, or de-aged without having to spend hours with the make-up and hairstyling teams. (Turn to page 102 to find out how CGI technology works with facial mapping.)

MOVIE FACT

In 2014, 20th Century Fox unsuccessfully campaigned for Andy Serkis to be nominated for an Oscar for his role in Dawn of the Planet of the Apes (2014) even though he physically didn't appear on screen.

89

SUPER STUNTS

Action, sci-fi, and fantasy films are packed with amazing stunts and thrilling sequences to wow the audience. Anything that is dangerous to film, or involves an element of risk, is called a stunt and created by highly skilled **stunt performers** and coordinators.

Early stunts

The first stunts were performed by comedians like Buster Keaton. His stunt from *Steamboat Bill, Jr.* (1928), where a house falls on him and he escapes unhurt, was very dangerous to film.

Buster remembered seeing the cameraman looking away, unable to watch, as the house fell on him!

Practice makes perfect

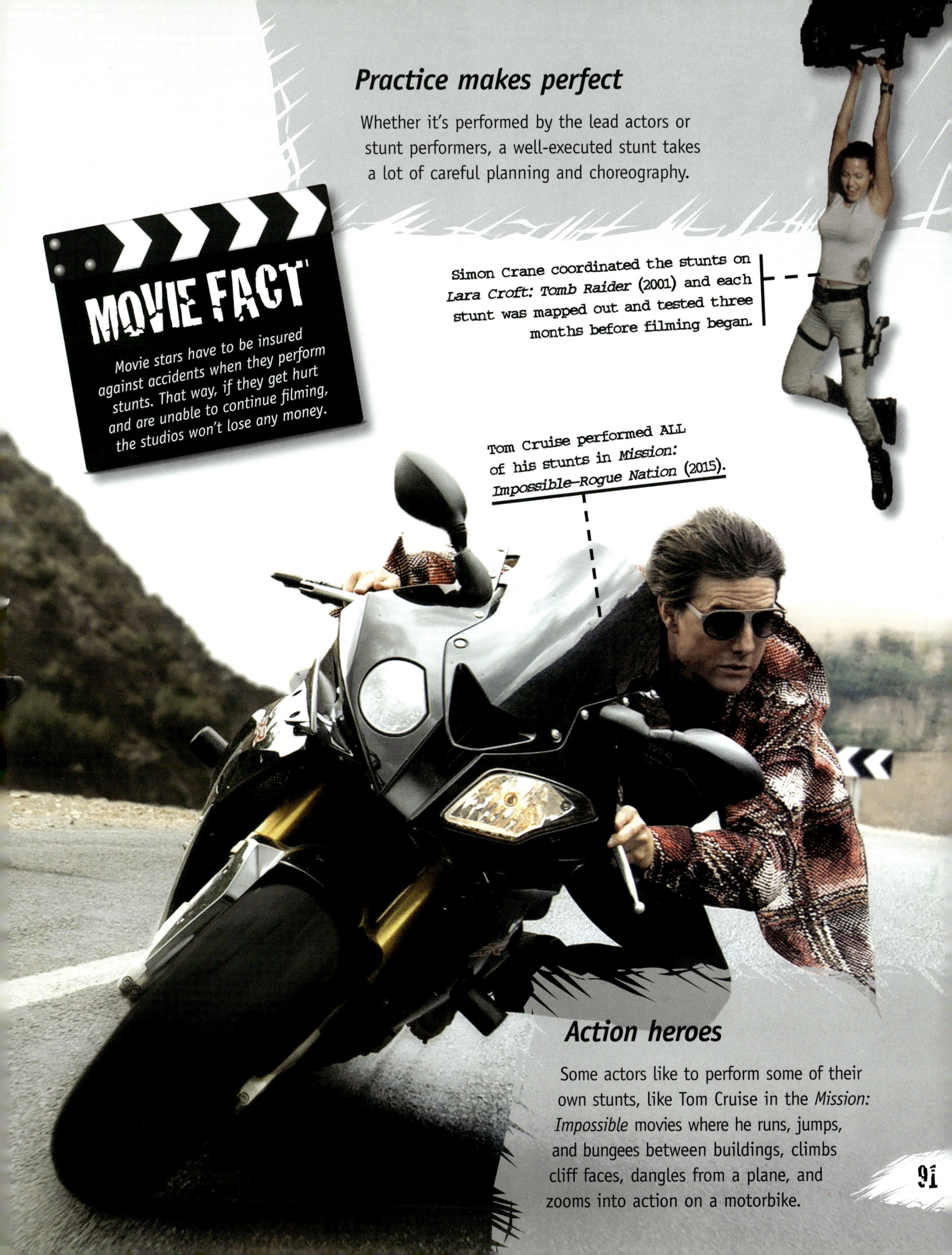

Whether it's performed by the lead actors or stunt performers, a well-executed stunt takes a lot of careful planning and choreography.

MOVIE FACT

Movie stars have to be insured against accidents when they perform stunts. That way, if they get hurt and are unable to continue filming, the studios won't lose any money.

Simon Crane coordinated the stunts on *Lara Croft: Tomb Raider* (2001) and each stunt was mapped out and tested three months before filming began.

Tom Cruise performed ALL of his stunts in *Mission: Impossible–Rogue Nation* (2015).

Action heroes

Some actors like to perform some of their own stunts, like Tom Cruise in the *Mission: Impossible* movies where he runs, jumps, and bungees between buildings, climbs cliff faces, dangles from a plane, and zooms into action on a motorbike.

STUNT PERFORMERS

One day they could be crashing a car, the next jumping from a plane! Every day is a totally unique experience for a movie stunt performer and they need to be in shape and know how to avoid injury.

Harrison Ford in Raiders of the Lost Ark (1981).

Stunt skills

Most successful stunt performers are also trained in at least two or more of the following skills...

Fighting stunts usually require martial arts and boxing skills.

Falling is harder than it looks, so a talent for trampolining and high diving is useful

Riding—being able to stay on a galloping horse at speed and control a motorcycle and car are a must!

Agility and strength are key and gymnastics comes in handy, plus being able to rock climb.

Swimming—being a good swimmer and trained in deep-sea diving all look good on the resume.

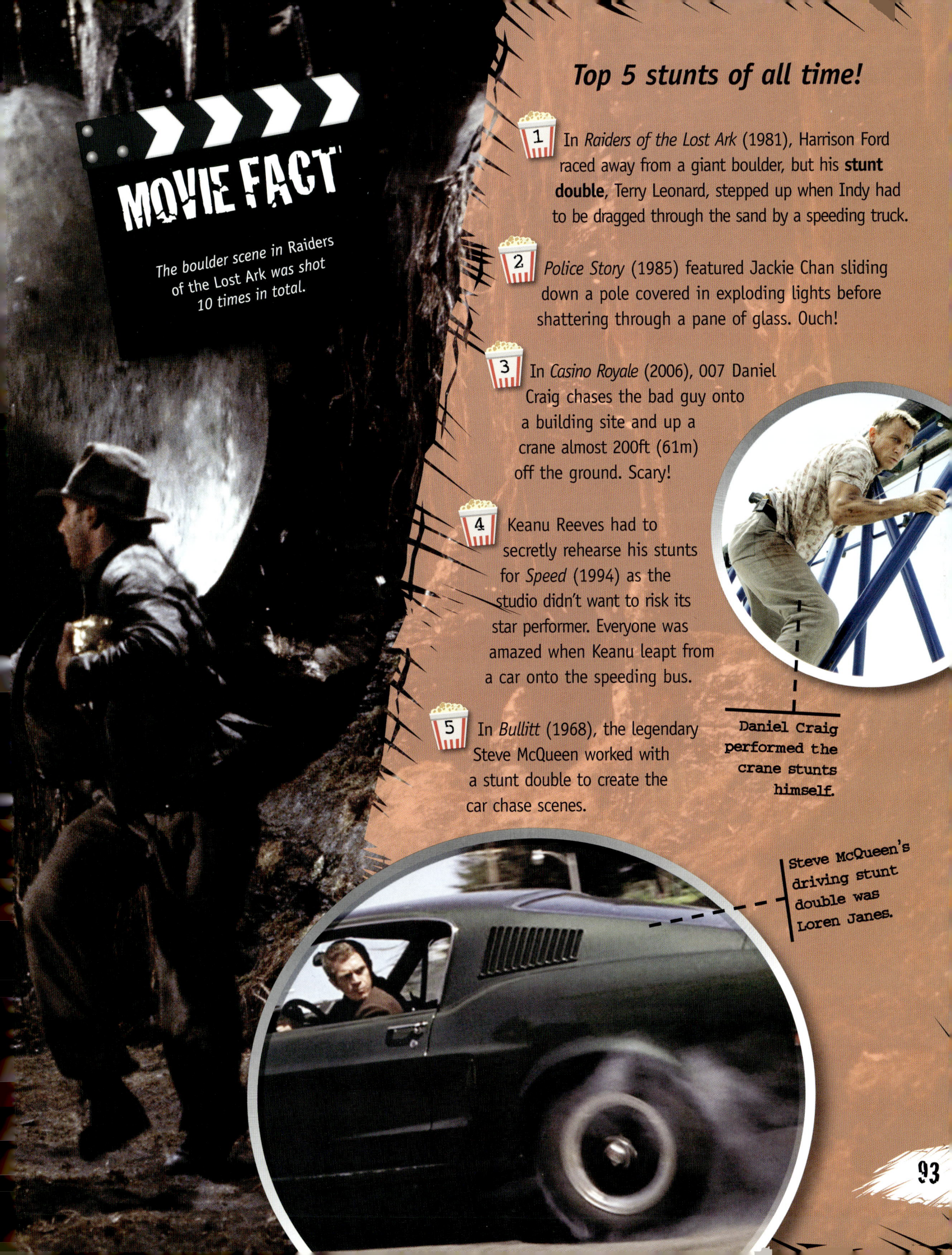

MOVIE FACT

The boulder scene in Raiders of the Lost Ark was shot 10 times in total.

Top 5 stunts of all time!

1. In *Raiders of the Lost Ark* (1981), Harrison Ford raced away from a giant boulder, but his **stunt double**, Terry Leonard, stepped up when Indy had to be dragged through the sand by a speeding truck.

2. *Police Story* (1985) featured Jackie Chan sliding down a pole covered in exploding lights before shattering through a pane of glass. Ouch!

3. In *Casino Royale* (2006), 007 Daniel Craig chases the bad guy onto a building site and up a crane almost 200ft (61m) off the ground. Scary!

4. Keanu Reeves had to secretly rehearse his stunts for *Speed* (1994) as the studio didn't want to risk its star performer. Everyone was amazed when Keanu leapt from a car onto the speeding bus.

5. In *Bullitt* (1968), the legendary Steve McQueen worked with a stunt double to create the car chase scenes.

Daniel Craig performed the crane stunts himself.

Steve McQueen's driving stunt double was Loren Janes.

93

POST-PRODUCTION

The post-production phase of creating a movie usually takes longer than the shooting of it. It can take anywhere from several months to several years to complete the editing, music, and sound effects.

MOVIE FACT

Quantel released The Harry, the first all-digital video editing and effects compositing system, in 1985.

The final edit

Once filming is finished, a picture and **sound editor** will create different drafts of the movie. From the first **rough cut** to the **final cut** and **answer print**, a director and producer have to view and approve the movie in several stages before it's ready to be distributed.

Show stoppers

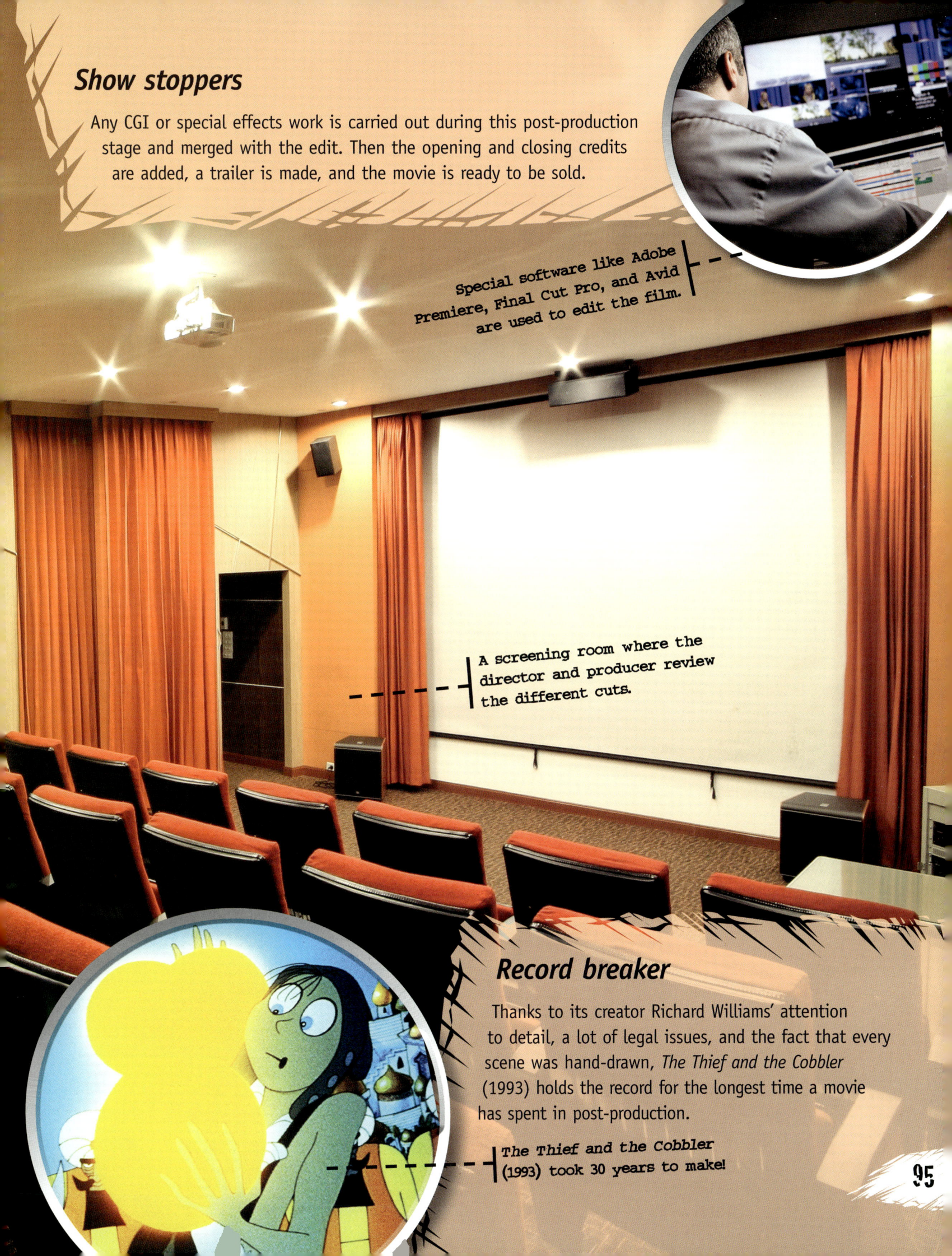

Any CGI or special effects work is carried out during this post-production stage and merged with the edit. Then the opening and closing credits are added, a trailer is made, and the movie is ready to be sold.

Special software like Adobe Premiere, Final Cut Pro, and Avid are used to edit the film.

A screening room where the director and producer review the different cuts.

Record breaker

Thanks to its creator Richard Williams' attention to detail, a lot of legal issues, and the fact that every scene was hand-drawn, *The Thief and the Cobbler* (1993) holds the record for the longest time a movie has spent in post-production.

The Thief and the Cobbler (1993) took 30 years to make!

EDITING SUITE

MOVIE FACT

Robert W. Paul's Come Along, Do! (1898) was one of the first movies to feature more than one shot.

Movie editing is a subtle craft. If it's good the viewer shouldn't notice it, if it's bad it can ruin a movie. A good film editor seeks to control the audience's mind by drawing them into the story and keeping them hooked till the credits roll.

Film and sound editor Walter Murch is known for his collaborations with Francis Ford Coppola on films like Apocalypse Now (1979).

How it's done

In the old days, editing was done with a positive copy of the film negative, called a **workprint**, which was literally cut and pasted together by the editor. Today, most films are edited digitally on systems like Avid or Final Cut Pro, which enable the editor to view clips in real time as they move them around.

Five steps to editing a movie

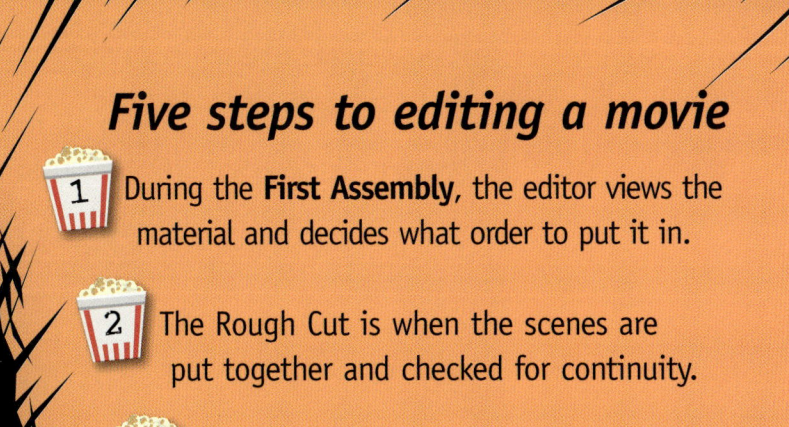

1. During the **First Assembly**, the editor views the material and decides what order to put it in.

2. The Rough Cut is when the scenes are put together and checked for continuity.

3. The First Cut is when the rough cut is approved and the sequence of scenes is fixed.

4. The Fine Cut no longer focuses on the entire movie, but each scene in detail.

5. The Final Cut is the final edit, when the sound effects and music are added.

Michael Kahn has three editing Oscars and worked with Steven Spielberg on *Saving Private Ryan* (1998).

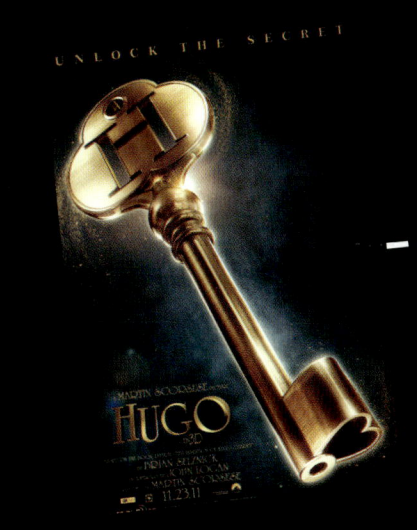

Thelma Schoonmaker has three Oscars and edited many of Martin Scorsese's movies including *Hugo* (2011).

EARLY VISUAL EFFECTS

Visual effects (also known as VFX) are the processes by which images are created outside of live-action shots in a movie. As soon as film makers figured out how to make movies, they began experimenting with visual effects, from animation and paintings to trick camera shots and models.

The city of London was painted by Jim Fetherolf for Mary Poppins (1964).

Painting a picture

Matte paintings were a vital part of many movies before CGI technology. These paintings were placed behind actors to trick audiences into believing the location was real.

A matte painting made the Emerald City sparkle in The Wizard of Oz (1939).

98

Model behavior

Movie makers often use models to create scenes, especially in sci-fi and fantasy franchises like the space stations and vehicles in the *Star Wars* movies and the Middle Earth locations in the *Lord of the Rings* trilogy.

George Melies' Trip to the Moon (1902) was the first movie to use models.

MOVIE FACT
Ub Iwerks, who was responsible for many of the amazing effects in Mary Poppins, is also famous for creating the final sketch design of Mickey Mouse.

Monster movers

A life-size Brontosaurus was built for the movie *The Lost World* (1925), which transported viewers back to prehistoric times. In *Jurassic Park* (1993), only 4 of the 14 minutes of the movie's dinosaur footage were rendered with computer graphics. The rest were filmed using **animatronic** models, including a huge T. rex and men in rubber velociraptor costumes.

99

VISUAL EFFECTS TODAY

Movie makers are always pushing the frontiers of new technology and creating more dazzling and spectacular special effects. As computers grow more powerful, so do the ways VFX teams use them.

Animated CGI

Disney joined forces with Pixar to release *Toy Story* (1995), the first feature-length animated movie created with CGI. The movie took four years to create, generated 1,000 gigabytes of data and took nearly 800,000 machine hours to edit.

John Lasseter directed *Toy Story* (1995) and is Chief Creative Officer of Pixar and Walt Disney Animation Studios.

Faking it

Today's VFXs are so realistic it's almost impossible to tell what's real and what's fake. In Ridley Scott's *The Martian* (2015), the VFX team actually blew up the Mars base on set, but created the visors for the space helmets in post-production.

Using CGI allowed the VFX team to control what was and wasn't reflected in the astronauts' visors.

MOVIE FACT

Tim Burton was still working on the movie Alice in Wonderland two weeks before its release.

Before and after

Many films are unrecognizable without their VFXs. The team behind *Alice in Wonderland* (2010) combined CGI with stilts, rubber rabbits, Nerf balls, and actors in green leotards to create the magical make-believe world conjured up for the big screen.

Helena Bonham Carter in *Alice in Wonderland* (2010).

101

CGI

A Computer Generated Image is an image that needs to be drawn, rendered, or created by a computer tool. CGI has revolutionized movies and is used to create all kinds of special effects, from backdrops to props or even the actors themselves.

Movie magic

Michael Crichton's *Westworld* (1973) was the first movie to use CGI effects. He employed John Whitney Jr. to undertake the work, which he completed in 4 months for $20,000.

Michael Crichton wrote and directed Westworld (1973).

MOVIE FACT

Industrial Light & Magic has worked on more than 300 movies and won an amazing 18 Best Visual Effects Oscars.

Leading light

For many years Industrial Light & Magic was the leading VFX company. Founded by George Lucas in 1975 for the first *Star Wars* movie, it was used by many studios to create CGI scenes and was the founding company of Pixar.

Game changers

The Matrix (1999) introduced dazzling new VFX like **"bullet time"** which involved filming a scene with lots of cameras at once, suspending actors on wires, then enhancing the scene with slow-motion digital sequencing and CGI.

"Bullet time" astonished audiences in 1999.

Tigers, thousands of extras, a historic Roman backdrop and even one of its deceased stars were conjured up for Gladiator (2000) using CGI

103

AMAZING ANIMATORS

Computer animators work using a brief from a director or lead animator to create designs, layouts, and models which they can then manipulate and move to create movie animation for the big screen.

Inventive idea

In 1963, Ivan Sutherland created an interactive drawing-and-design program called Sketchpad while studying at the Massachusetts Institute of Technology. This paved the way for more computer animation programs which developed into a billion-dollar industry.

Tools of the trade

Many of the basic tools of CGI were developed between 1975 and 1983 and, during this time, the increase in computer power and design enabled artists who didn't have any previous computer experience or qualifications to work and create with them.

Types of animation

1. 3D animation involves building 3D models that can be manipulated and moved to create an animated scene, as in *Madagascar* (2005).

2. 2D animation is traditional two-dimensional animations, with one drawing followed by another in a slightly different pose to create movement, as in *Spirited Away* (2001).

3. Stop-motion animation involves taking a photograph of an object or character, moving it slightly, then taking another photograph to merge together, as used in *Fantastic Mr. Fox* (2009) and *Shaun the Sheep* (2015).

Madagascar (2005).

Spirited Away (2001).

Fantastic Mr. Fox (2009).

21 Shaun puppets were made for *Shaun the Sheep Movie* (2015).

MOVIE FACT

CGI movie Toy Story (1995) was a huge achievement considering half of its crew had never used a computer before working on it.

ANIMATION STUDIOS

The animation industry today is worth billions of dollars. Despite taking huge teams to creatively produce an animated movie, it's still one of the most profitable genres at the box office, with studios from Disney to Dreamworks all cashing in.

MOVIE FACT

Studio executives weren't convinced Snow White and the Seven Dwarfs (1937) was going to be a success and nicknamed it "Disney's Folly."

Pencil pioneers

For many, the animation industry began with Walt Disney. He created one of the first animation studios, The Walt Disney Studio, in 1926, with his brother Roy. Their first hand-drawn animation *Steamboat Willie* (1926) introduced Mickey Mouse to the world.

The Disney HQ, in Burbank, California, looks like it's held up by the seven dwarves.

Walt Disney has won the most Oscars, with 22 awards.

Box-office smashers

1. *Snow White and the Seven Dwarfs* (1937) was the first feature-length animated color movie, released in 1937.

2. *Spirited Away* (2001) broke box-office records in Japan in 2001 and won an Oscar for Best Animated Feature.

3. *Chicken Run* (2000) is the most successful stop-motion animation movie and made more than $224 million at the box office.

Biggest animation studios

1. Industrial Light & Magic's hits include *Pacific Rim* (2013) and the *Transformers* movies.

2. Framestore created animations and effects for *The Golden Compass* (2007) and *Harry Potter and the Deathly Hallows* (2010).

3. Moving Picture Company helped animate *Godzilla* (2014), *The Life of Pi* (2012), and *Skyfall* (2012).

4. Double Negative brought the amazing animations in *Batman vs Superman: Dawn of Justice* (2016) and *Jupiter Ascending* (2015) to the big screen.

5. Walt Disney Animation Studios may be an oldie, but it's still a goodie, churning out a stream of box-office hits like *Frozen* (2013), *Big Hero 6* (2014), and *Zootopia* (2016).

Godzilla (2014).

Pacific Rim (2013).

Frozen (2013).

AMAZING AUDIO

A **sound designer** begins their work on a movie during the planning stages. They then work with the director in the production and post-production stages to create a soundtrack for the movie that can include all kinds of sounds, from the actors' dialogue to sound effects and a musical soundtrack.

MOVIE FACT

Movie makers often look to source additional sounds from libraries like Sound Ideas, Sounddogs, and Sonniss.

Audio recognition

The role of the sound designer emerged in the early 1970s, with Francis Ford Coppola recognizing Walter Murch's work on his movie *Apocalypse Now* (1979), where he created all aspects of the audio, from the recording to re-recording and final mixing of all sounds.

Most movie makers use a digital audio workstation or DAW, which allows sounds to be stored, mixed, and manipulated as computer files.

Apocalypse Now was recorded using the Dolby Stereo 70mm six track system.

Iconic sound

Sound designer Ben Burtt realized that what a movie audience hears enhances what they see and took this into consideration when creating his famous *Star Wars* sounds, including R2-D2's beeps, the lightsaber hum, and the blasts of the blaster guns.

Darth Vader's menacing breathing was made by recording the sound of breathing into a scuba regulator.

SOUND SOLUTIONS

The post-production sound process involves **dubbing**, Automatic Dialogue Recording, and subtitles, then merging all elements together to create a final soundtrack for the movie.

MOVIE FACT

Sometimes dubbing is used for songs. Marni Nixon's voice was used to fix glitches in Natalie Wood's songs in West Side Story (1961).

Dubbing

Dubbing is when a foreign-language audio is dubbed onto a movie's soundtrack to translate the movie's original soundtrack for a new and foreign audience. The skill is matching the new audio to the lip movements of the actors in the movie.

Additional dialogue recording

Additional dialogue recording (ADR) describes the process when an actor is called back to re-record their dialogue in a sound studio to achieve a cleaner sound or perhaps deliver their lines in a different way.

Amy Poehler recording her lines for Free Birds (2013).

Subtitles

Most foreign movies are shown with subtitles, as audiences prefer to hear the original language of a movie, which adds to its atmosphere. Subtitles are usually created with computer software, which helps the subtitles appear and disappear at exactly the right time to match the dialogue on screen.

Crouching Tiger Hidden Dragon (2008) was a huge subtitled hit, winning the Oscar for Best Foreign Language movie.

iii

MUSIC MASTERPIECES

From a time when the Romans used music to accompany their plays, to the first time the Lumière brothers played music with their early motion pictures, drama and music have always been linked. Movie makers today enhance the action and create their musical soundtracks either with existing songs or tunes especially composed for their movies.

Top scores

Accomplished **composers** are hired to create music that will appeal to the audiences and enhance a story. Max Steiner was one of the early greats, composing catchy and moving music for *King Kong* (1933), *Gone with the Wind* (1939), and *The Charge of the Light Brigade* (1936).

MOVIE FACT

Max Steiner's compositions were nominated for Oscars 24 times and he won 3 awards for The Informer (1935), Now Voyager (1942), and Since You Went Away (1944).

Music marvels

A soundtrack can either refer to everything you hear in a movie or just the songs created or licensed for it. The Oscars recognizes both the best Original Score and Original Song when awarding its award statues.

Adele got an Original Song Oscar for Skyfall (2013) and her song helped dramatize and promote the movie.

John Williams conducting the the score for Star Wars: Episode II Attack of the Clones (2002).

Hit factory

Movie makers have long realized the bonus of providing a chart-topping hit or theme song to accompany their movie. Sometimes just hearing a few notes can make someone think of a particular movie and, more importantly, make them want to watch it.

1. Bryan Adams sold 15 million copies of his *Robin Hood: Prince of Thieves* (1991) hit *Everything I Do (I Do it for You)*.

2. Rocky punched along to the fighting beats of *Eye of the Tiger* in 1982, with the song topping the charts for six weeks in the US.

3. Destiny's Child had a No. 1 hit with the song *Independent Women Part 1* for the movie *Charlie's Angels* (2000).

Former lead singer of Destiny's Child, Beyonce Knowles-Carter.

113

TITLE SEQUENCES

Hooking an audience right from the start is an important part of movie making. An exciting opening title sequence sets the tone for the entire movie and needs to make a strong first impression that will keep the audience in their seats and their eyes glued to the screen.

Early openers

Early black-and-white movies were opened with simple title cards showing the movie's name and some credits. These soon developed to more unusual and elaborate sequences and by the 1950s the sequences were a showboat for the latest designs and animation.

Early titles were often accompanied by music, too.

MOVIE FACT

The opening credits for The Fugitive (1993) continued over several opening scenes, and did not finish until 15 minutes into the movie.

Sequence superstars

Saul Bass created title sequences for some of the biggest movie makers, including Alfred Hitchcock, Martin Scorsese, and Stanley Kubrick. He used innovative techniques from cut-out animations to striking typography. He liked to make the ordinary extraordinary.

Title sequence creator Saul Bass also designed company logos and iconic movie posters, like this one for Vertigo (1958).

3 classic openers

Some movie openers stand out from the rest, setting up the story and building anticipation of what is to come.

1 Few opening sequences set up a story as well as *Back to the Future*'s (1985) slow pan shot around scientist Doc Brown's lab, filled with time gadgets and stolen plutonium.

2 *The Lion King* (1994) captivated its viewers with a powerful and moving opening animation and an even more powerful and moving song.

3 A long time ago, in a galaxy far, far away... George Lucas' golden crawling text hooked the viewer in and gave themsome useful backstory at the same time.

The original Star Wars title logo is still used today for its movies and merchandise.

115

CLOSING CREDITS

A movie's credits are a list of everyone involved with the movie production and appear at the end of a movie, usually in small type. They usually either flip very quickly from page to page, or move slowly across a plain background.

Stuart, Kevin, and Bob play with a young Gru at the end of Minions (2015) during the credits.

The End

Early credits often just consisted of some text, telling the audience the movie had ended.

That's all folks!

It wasn't until the early 1970s that credits became a regular feature at the end of a movie. Before then, only the main actors and crew were credited for their parts in a production and this was usually at the start of the movie.

Big productions

Today, never-ending credit rolls have become more common, especially in movies with lots of special effects. *Iron Man 3* (2013) credits more than 3,300 people.

The Hunger Games: Mockingjay Part 1 (2014) had a whopping 12 minutes of credits.

MOVIE FACT

In Ferris Bueller's Day Off (1986), Ferris pops back up during the credits to say "You're still here? It's over! Go home!"

Bloopers

To make credits more entertaining, extra scenes or **bloopers** (scenes that have gone wrong) are often added. Sometimes the movie's characters appear and interact with the credits.

DISTRIBUTION

Movie distribution relates to everything that happens between a movie's production and when it's shown on the big or small screen. It's a process that involves all the deals done to get the movie promoted, sold, and seen by the biggest audience, in as many different formats as possible.

What does a distributor do?

A distribution company is responsible for: getting the movie out to the audience, obtaining certifications from the regulation bodies, arranging the movie's screenings around the world, and selling the TV and DVD rights.

A distributor also creates posters and video clips to help publicize the movie.

Many of the world's biggest distributors are based in Los Angeles, in the U.S.

Main distributors

United International, Warner Bros., Buena Vista, 20th Century Fox, and Sony distribute more than 90% of the movies shown today. These companies are often directly linked to the main Hollywood companies who make their movies, like Buena Vista, which is owned by The Walt Disney Company.

MOVIE FACT

James Cameron's movies Avatar (2009) and Titanic (1997) hold the top two spots for most-watched movies around the world.

Distribution deals

Vertical distribution is when the production company has ownership of all elements, from the movie's production to the distribution and exhibition, and receives all the profit. Warner Bros. is an example of this, being able to produce, distribute, and show its movies without any other company being involved.

BUILDING THE HYPE

The internet has transformed the way a movie is promoted. Distributors build awareness of a movie before its release, with trailing posts, images, and video clips to tease the audience and get them excited about the movie.

The trailer for *Star Wars: The Force Awakens* (2015) was seen online 128 million times within 24 hours of its release!

Teasers

During filming, the creators will release an increasing flow of information about the movie via the press and social media to engage with the potential audience and make them feel like a part of the movie before its release.

Distributors built anticipation for *Warcraft* (2016) by showing early footage at the San Diego Comic Con.

Trailer

A trailer is the most cost-effective marketing tool, as it can be played on both the big screen, before other movies, to a captive audience, and also online. A trailer is carefully crafted to showcase its own mini story, including the best parts of the movie, without giving too much away.

MOVIE FACT

The Golden Trailer Awards has 82 categories, including the Golden Fleece Award, given to the best movie trailer where the marketing was considered better than the movie itself.

Maximum impact

Trailers are so important that a distributor will usually hire an independent trailer specialist, like Wild Card, Trailer Park, or Buddha Jones, to create it.

Trailers now receive their own Golden Trailer Awards to celebrate their brilliance. The first awards were held in 1999.

THE ROAD TO SUCCESS

Once a movie is finished and its distribution deals are done, the distribution company sets about scheduling a release date, getting it rated, and starting up the marketing machine to sell, sell, sell!

Perfect timing

Standard release dates are set to prevent different elements of a movie's distribution from competing with each other. A movie will be released in the theater first, then on DVD (around 16 weeks after its theater release), and finally at home via TV (anything 7up to two years after its theater-release date).

Buena Vista Home Entertainment releases its Disney-movies under the brand name Disney Blu-ray.

Posters advertising movies are displayed in theaters, shopping malls, on the sides of buildings and buses, and at airports and stations.

Ratings

Every motion picture is given a **rating** to determine its suitability for a particular audience. In some countries, like Australia, the rating is awarded by an official government system, while in the U.S. it's done by an industry committee.

Marketing

Once the rating has been established and the release dates agreed, a movie marketing machine begins to promote the movie in all kinds of media, from TV, internet, and print advertising to merchandising and promotional tours for its actors.

Actors give press interviews to help promote the movies they star in, like Al Pacino interviewing here with Xpose.

MOVIE FACT

Sometimes, but not often, a movie is released simultaneously at the theater and on DVD. It can also go straight to DVD and skip the theater screening altogether.

MOVIE RELEASE

As a movie's release date gets closer, the movie marketeers go into overdrive to create positive press coverage in print, online, and on TV. The main focus is around a press **junket**, but can also involve other ways to promote a movie, from a **premiere** to a publicity stunt.

Press junket

For a big blockbuster movie, journalists and movie **critics** are all flown to one special location for a day or weekend to interview the movie's main stars and creators and discover all there is to know about the movie.

It's easy to spot when an actor or director is being interviewed at a press junket as they're usually sitting in front of a poster for their movie.

Sneak peek

The first showing of a movie is called the premiere, which plays a big part in generating interest in a movie. The movie's main stars and crew attend premieres all over the world, usually in capital cities, where critics and VIPs (very important people) can watch the movie.

Fans pose for selfies with George Clooney at a premiere.

Stunt tactics

A **publicity stunt** is a specially organized event, where someone (usually an actor from the movie) does something really silly, dangerous, or spectacular to draw further attention to the movie's opening.

Daniel Craig arriving at the *Spectre* (2015) London premiere.

MOVIE FACT

For Independence Day (1996) a fake news broadcast, reporting an alien invasion, aired during the Superbowl. This led to a lot of publicity for the movie, but also to many terrified viewers dialling 911!

125

MOVIE THEATERS

Around 1.2 billion movie theater tickets are sold each year in the US. Most of the money a movie theater makes from selling tickets goes straight back to the studio though, leaving little profit for the theater owners themselves.

Split sales

The percentage distributors take reduces each week until the movie run is over. This means theaters usually only make money on the big blockbuster movies that draw large crowds for a long time.

Distributors take around 80% of ticket sales for the first few weeks a movie is shown.

The average cost of a movie ticket in the US is $8.43.

Popcorn profits

Theaters make most of their money selling popcorn, hotdogs, ice cream, candy, and soft drinks to their customers.

Snacks at theaters come in large sizes and can be expensive!

MOVIE FACT

AMC became the biggest movie theater chain in the U.S. when it bought Carmike Cinemas in 2016, adding 2,500 theaters to its own 2,000.

Ad sales

Movie theaters also make money by showing movie trailers and displaying posters, too. Distributors base their payments to theater owners on how many people have seen their promotions.

Theaters have to report how many customers they've had before they get paid.

FAMOUS THEATERS

Most movie fans agree that the best place to experience a movie is on the big screen. Movie theaters are constantly developing to create amazing experiences for their customers and ones they can't recreate at home.

Biggest to the best

The 540-seat IMAX screen in Sydney, Australia, is the largest in the world. Viewers are treated to a screen that's 117 feet wide and 96 feet high, while the Nokia Ultra Screen in Bangkok, Thailand, offers its customers reclining seats, free snacks in the VIP lounge, and a foot massage. The Rooftop Curtain Cinema in Melbourne, Australia has 185 relaxing deck chairs from which you can marvel at the movie and the view.

The Rooftop Curtain Cinema in Melbourne, Australia.

The IMAX theater in Sydney, Australia.

Oldest to the comfiest

The world's oldest theater is l'Eden Theatre in La Ciotat, France, where the pioneering Lumière brothers screened their first motion picture in 1899. The Electric Theatre in London, England, could be the comfiest, with leather armchairs, sofas, and double beds from which to watch its movies. It also hands out cashmere blankets for those who want to get really cozy.

MOVIE FACT

There are around 39,000 indoor and 595 drive-in movie theaters in the U.S.

Drive-in theaters were very popular in the 1950s, with more than 4,000 across the U.S.

The spookiest

If you're looking for a different kind of movie experience, the film group Cinespia hosts movie nights at the Hollywood Forever Cemetery, so you can watch a movie sitting among the gravestones. Guaranteed to give you goosebumps!

Movie night at Hollywood Forever Cemetery.

129

HOME MOVIES

Thanks to computer technology, distributors can sell movies in all kinds of formats that people can watch in the comfort of their own homes. From the early videos to the latest streaming apps, it's possible to watch movies via computers, TV, and phones.

MOVIE FACT

Peter Jackson's Director's Cut of The Lord of the Rings series took what was already considered a very long trilogy and extended it to a 12-hour version.

Changing formats

The first VHS recorders, which played movies on a video cassette, were sold in the 1970s. By 2002, the DVD format was outselling VHS and 90% of people owned a DVD player. Thanks to an increasing internet bandwidth, streaming became widely available in the early 2000s, too.

VHS is short for Video Home System.

Hidden extras

The storage space on a DVD disc, or specially created apps and websites, enables movie makers to give their customers more for their money, with bonus extras like interviews, behind-the-scenes footage, or different versions of the movie, like a Director's Cut.

Five different versions of the movie Blade Runner (1982) are included in a special Ultimate Collector's disc.

Most home theaters have a large screen, several speakers, and comfy seats.

Movie night

Home-theater equipment is constantly improving with amazing sound and screen technology. Jeremy Kipnis devoted three years and $6 million to create the world's largest and loudest home theater in his home in Connecticut.

AWARDS SEASON

By hosting a series of awards around the world each year, the movie industry likes to celebrate the best movies made and recognize everyone who worked on them. These awards also help promote the movies to the distributors and audiences.

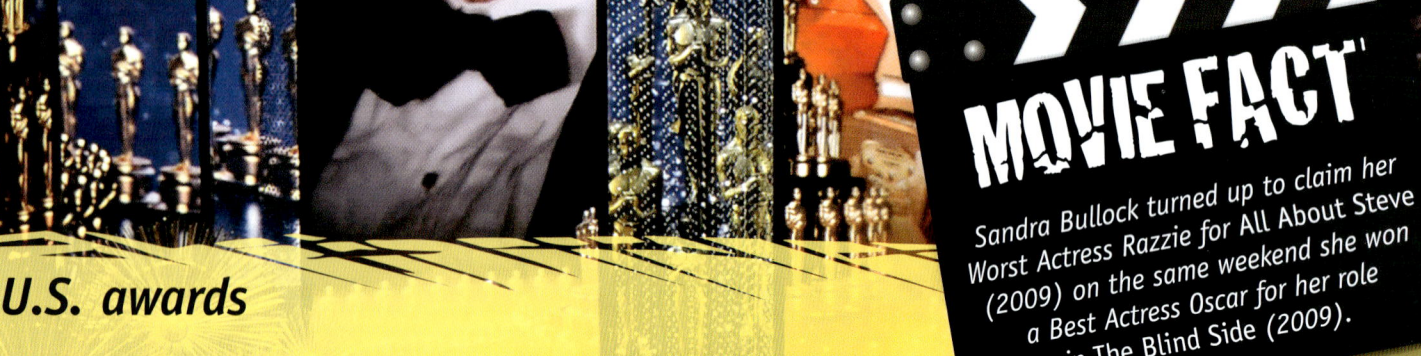

MOVIE FACT

Sandra Bullock turned up to claim her Worst Actress Razzie for All About Steve (2009) on the same weekend she won a Best Actress Oscar for her role in The Blind Side (2009).

U.S. awards

The U.S. has many award ceremonies, mostly held between November and January. Here are the top three:

Award: Golden Globes
When it began: 1947
Who votes: Members of the Hollywood Foreign Press Association
Did you know?: Meryl Streep has won 7 Golden Globes for her starring roles.

Award: Academy Awards
When it began: 1929
Who votes: Around 600 members of the Academy.
Did you know?: Due to a metal shortage during World War II, the Oscar statues were made of plaster for 3 years.

Award: Golden Raspberries
When it began: 1981
Who votes: Anyone who has paid $40 for a Razzie membership.
Did you know?: These awards celebrate the worst movies and actors.

Julianne Moore announcing the winner of the Best Actor Award at the 2016 Oscar ceremony.

UK awards

The BAFTAs is the largest UK ceremony.

Award: BAFTAs
When it began: 1948
Who votes: 6,500 members of the BAFTA. The public votes for the Rising Star Award.
Did you know?: BAFTA has awards for 25 different film-related categories.

John Boyega received the Rising Star BAFTA in 2016.

Worldwide awards

There are also a number of award ceremonies held around the world. Two of the biggest are:

Award: European Film Academy
When it began: 1988
Who votes: Members of the European Film Academy.
Did you know?: The awards are in Berlin every second year, and elsewhere in Europe in between.

Award: Filmfare Awards, India
When it began: 1954
Who votes: Voted for by the public and a committee.
Did you know?: The Filmfare Awards are the oldest in India.

FESTIVAL FUN

The movie industry uses **festivals** to promote movies around the world. Lots of movies are shown, movie stars parade down red carpets posing for pictures and giving interviews, and, behind the scenes, deals are done and millions are made.

Screenings at the Venice Film Festival take place in the historic Palazzo del Cinema.

Golden oldie

The Venice Film Festival is the world's oldest and was founded in 1932. The festival presents several awards including the Golden Lion, for the best movie, and the Silver Lion for the best director.

Big in Berlin

The Berlinale is the largest public film festival, with more than 300,000 tickets available to fans. The best movie wins the coveted Golden Bear award.

In 2015, 441 films were shown over 10 days at the Berlinale.

Emma Stone, Woody Allen, and Parker Posey on the red carpet in Cannes, 2015.

Fun in the sun

The first Cannes Film Festival's launch was delayed when World War II broke out in 1939, and didn't take place till 1946. The Palme d'Or is Canne's most important award and is given to the favorite movie of the year.

MOVIE FACT

The red carpet is changed three times a day during the Cannes Film Festival.

135

MAKE YOUR OWN MOVIE

Whether you want to become an actor or just have a great story you want to share with the world, it's easy to make your own movie. All you need is a great idea, some movie-making equipment, and a lot of time and patience.

You can also download free software to create a music soundtrack.

What you'll need:

1. An idea for your movie—better yet, a full script.

2. Actors to act in it. Friends and family will do if you can't afford any pros.

3. A phone or camera for filming.

4. A computer to edit your videos on.

5. Software to edit your videos. Movie Maker or iMovie are free and easy to use.

6. Good lighting is essential. See page 82 for how to set up basic lighting.

7. Sound is also important, so check out page 84 for some handy hints.

8. Time and dedication.

What you do:

1. Once your script is created, think about where you want to film the scenes, find a location, and plan out what you'll need to shoot each of them.

2. Once your movie is shot, spend a lot of time editing it so it's perfect. Add special effects and ensure the sound is good.

3. If you can't do everything yourself, network to chat with other movie makers. Websites like shootingpeople.org and raindance.org are good places to start, but be sure to ask a grown-up before going online.

You can shoot your movie on any kind of recording device, from a digital camera to your mobile phone.

Getting it out there:

1. There are no shortcuts to getting your movie seen and paid for by an audience. The process can often be as hard, if not tougher, than making the movie itself.

2. Submit your movie to festivals or competitions to help raise awareness.

3. Organize your own small screenings in local theaters, schools, or gyms.

4. Upload a trailer to YouTube or Vimeo. Make sure you ask a grown-up before going online and setting up an account.

5. For a VOD or pay-per-view option, release it via Amazon's Create Space or Vimeo Pro.

6. Send it to a TV network for release on the small screen only.

GLOSSARY

agent
A person who represents an actor.

actor
A male or female who plays (acts) a character in a movie.

Automatic Dialogue Replacement (ADR)
The re-recording of dialog in a studio, to replace that recorded on set.

animatic
An animated storyboard.

animation
The technique of creating a succession of images or positions of models, to create the illusion of movement.

animatronics
Robotic models used to imitate a human, animal, or other object to bring them to life.

answer print
A motion-picture film print composed of picture and sound and used for review.

art director
A person who is in charge of the design of a movie set and how it looks and feels.

assistant director
A person who helps the director on a movie.

audition
When an actor tries out for a role in a movie.

backdrop
The background of a scene. Usually a large painting or, in CGI movies, a green screen.

backlot
An outside space in a movie studio, used for filming outside scenes.

behind the scenes
The off-camera events during filming.

best boy/girl
First assistant to the gaffer or grip.

blockbuster
A movie that makes a lot of money at the box office, usually more than $200 million.

blocking
When actors mark out their positions, before filming their scenes.

blooper
A mistake in a scene that is sometimes shown at the end of a movie for laughs.

boom operator
Person who holds the boom, which holds the microphone.

breakdown sheet
A sheet containing details of a scene for filming.

budget
The costs of making a movie.

bullet time
A visual effect where time is slowed so the viewer can see bullets flying through the air.

CAD
Computer-aided design.

call sheet
An information sheet given to cast and crew to let them know where to be for filming.

casting director
The person who finds the right actors and assigns them roles in a movie.

CGI
Computer-generated images, used to create special effects characters and locations.

chroma key
The process when actors are shot in front of a green screen so they can be separated from their background.

cinematographer
The person in charge of selecting the right lighting and cameras and capturing the images.

clapperboard (slate)
Used to label a scene and take at the beginning of each shot. Also used to help synchronize the sound when the movie is edited.

composer
The person who creates the movie's musical score.

computer animator
A person who creates animations on a computer.

costumes
Any garments worn by actors during filming.

costume designer
The person who designs the costumes.

credits
A list of all cast and crew involved in creating a movie.

critic
A person who writes and comments on a movie in the media.

development
The process of putting all elements in place to make a movie.

director
A person in artistic control of the movie and responsible for directing the cast and crew.

director of photography
A person in artistic control of filming the movie.

distributor
A person or company that sells the movie and ensures it's seen by an audience.

dubbing
The process of replacing audio on a movie's soundtrack.

editing
The process of selecting and fitting together shots filmed to make a movie.

executive producer
A person in charge of a movie's financing.

extra
A person who appears in a movie in a non-speaking role.

facial mapping
Technology used to superimpose one actor's face on another's body.

feedback
Audience opinion, following early cuts of a movie.

festival
An event where movies can be premiered, awarded, and promoted to create distribution deals.

final cut
The last edit of a movie and how it will be seen.

First Assembly
The editor views all the material from the movie and and decides what order to put it in.

foley artist
An actor who creates sound effects like kissing, footsteps, and punching during post production.

franchise
A series of movies that have been created from one original story, concept, or brand.

gaffer
The person in charge of lighting on a movie set.

greenlit
When a movie gets the go-ahead and is put into production.

grip
The person in charge of the equipment that holds the lighting, cameras, and microphones.

green screen
A green screen which actors are filmed against, so they can then be merged with computer-generated backgrounds.

hairstylist
Person in charge of hair design on a movie.

hero prop
A prop that will be filmed in close up.

IMAX
A larger-than-normal movie theater with a huge screen and amazing surround sound.

junket
A press event to promote a movie.

location
Where a movie is shot.

location scout
A person who finds a location to shoot a movie.

logline
A short sentence that sums up what a movie is about.

make-up artist
A person who is in charge of the make-up on a movie.

pitch
Presenting an idea for a movie.

post-production
The stage following the filming of a movie.

premiere
The first official movie screening.

pre-production
The planning stage of making a movie.

press manager
The person in charge of promoting a movie.

producer
The person who is in charge of the budget, logistics, and scheduling of a movie.

production
The stage when filming takes place.

production designer
A person responsible for bringing a director's vision to the screen.

props
Moveable objects used by actors during filming.

prop master
A person who designs and makes the props.

publicity stunt
Event created to promote a movie.

rating
Where different countries award a movie a rating, based on who the movie is suitable for.

rights
Ownership of the story of a movie and its rights.

rough cut
An early cut or edit of a movie, before it is finalized for viewing.

screening
A showing of a movie on a screen to a particular audience, this could be the cast and crew, critics, or a focus group to research how an audience reacts to a movie.

screenplay/script
A word document written for a movie, with all the words spoken and actors' movements described.

sets
The backdrop and surroundings a scene is filmed against.

set designer
A person who designs movie sets.

sound assistant
A person who assists the sound team on a movie.

sound designer
A person who designs and helps create the sounds on a movie.

sound editor
A person who edits the sounds on a movie.

soundstage
A large soundproof area used for filming.

soundtrack
Contains all the sound heard on a movie.

special effects
Sound and visual effects created to enhance a movie.

storyboard
A series of illustrations that outline the shots needed to translate the script into a scene.

studio
Companies that finance, create, and distribute movies.

stunt
An unusual and difficult physical feat or an act requiring a special skill.

stunt performer/double
A performer who takes the place of an actor in scenes that they don't want to undertake, like dangerous stunt scenes.

subtitles
Text that appears on screen to tell the audience what is being said in a movie.

trailer
A short version of the movie, designed to make the audience want to watch it.

treatment
The idea of a movie, written as a story with lots of detail.

unit production manager
A person who oversees the entire movie production.

vertical distribution
When a company can both create and distribute a movie.

visual effects
Imagery created outside the main shot.

workprint
A rough version of a movie.

INDEX

Abrams, JJ 38
Academy Awards 132
Adams, Bryan 113
additional dialogue recording 111,
Adele 113
Affleck, Ben 37, 61
AMC 127
arc shot 20
aerial shot 20
animation studios 106-7
art director 52
assistant director 53
Atlas studios 12
awards 132-3, 134, 135

Bad Robot Productions 38
BAFTAs 133
Baker, Rick 64
Bass, Saul 115
Berlinale 135
Besson, Luc 13
best boy/girl 54
Bollywood 13
Bonham Carter, Helena 100-1
Bray, Ann 65
breakdown sheets 69
bridging shot 20
Brigadoon 81
budget 16
Buena Vista 119, 122
Bullitt 93
Bullock, Sandra 81
Burton, Tim 101
Burtt, Ben 109

cail sheets 72
camera assistants 74
camera operator 74
cameras 78-9
Cameron, William 44
Cannes Film Festival 134, 135
Cannom, Greg 63

casting 48-9
CGI 22, 39, 95, 100, 101, 102-5
Chan, Jackie 14, 93
Chaplin, Charlie 35
Cher 61
Christian, Roger 45
chroma keying 86
Cinecitta studio 13
cinematographer 80-1
cinematography 20-1, 78-9, 80-1
clapperboard 73, 74
close up 20
closing credits 116-7
Columbia Pictures 28
Coppola, Francis Ford 109
costume designer 17, 60-1
Craig, Daniel 93, 124-5
Crane, Simon 91
Cruise, Tom 61, 91

dailies 75
Damon, Matt 37
Deakins, Roger 51
deep focus 20
Destiny's Child 113
Diesel, Vin 14
director 51, 71, 75
director of photography 51
Disney, Walt 46-7, 106
distribution 118-9
Docter, Pete 37
dolly zoom 20
double negative 107
Downey Jr., Robert 14-5
dubbing 110
Dudman, Nick 62
Dunst, Kirsten 64-5
Dutch tilt 20
DVDs 122, 123, 130, 131

Eastman, George 8
Eden Theater 129
Edison, Thomas 8, 10, 26, 83
editing 19, 96-7
Electric Theater 129
establishing shot 21

European Film Academy 133
executive producer 50
extras 49

Fetherolf, Jim 98
Fiennes, Ralph 62-3
Film City studio 13
film festivals 134-5
Filmfare Awards 133
final cut 19
financing movies 32-3
Ford, Harrison 92-3
Framestore studio 107
France 13

G Star soundstage 77
gaffer 54, 83
genres 24-5
Golden Bear 135
Golden Globes 132
Golden Lion 134
Golden Raspberries 132
Golden Trailer Awards 121
Grant, Cary 58-9
green screen 86-7
Griffith, DW 10
grip 54

hairstyling 64-5
Hammer, Armie 89
handheld 21
Hanks, Tom 34, 50
Harris, Neil Patrick 15
Head, Edith 60
Hepburn, Audrey 65
Hepburn, Katharine 15
Higgins, John 83
high angle 21
Hollywood Forever Cemetery 129
home-movie making 136-7
Home-theater
  equipment 130-1

IMAX 23, 128
IMAX theater 128-9
India 13
Industrial Light and Magic 102-3
Italy 13
Iwerks, Ub 99

Jackson, Peter 39
Japan 13
Jobs, Steve 39

Kahn, Michael 97
Keaton, Buster 90
Kipnis, Jeremy 131
Koepp, David 35

La Cité du Cinéma studio 13
Lang, Charles 81
Lawrence, Jennifer 15, 48
Leonard, Terry 93
lighting 82-3, 87
location scout 56
locations 56-7, 70
locked-down 21
logline 35
long shot 21
Lopez, Jennifer 15
low angle 21
Lumière brothers 8, 9, 112, 129

make-up 62-3
Makovsky, Judianna 61
Manley, Nellie 65
Marshall, Rob 72
matte paintings 98
McQueen, Steve 18, 93
medium shot 21
Melies, George 99
MGM studios 11, 27
Miyazaki 13
money shot 21
Monroe, Marilyn 27
Moretz, Chloë Grace 48
movie development 30-1
movie set 72-3
movie theaters 126-7, 128-9
Moving Picture Company 107
Murch, Walter 109
music 112-3
Muybridge, Eadweard 9

Nestor studio 10
Nicholson, Jack 15
Nixon, Marnie 110
Nokia Ultra Screen 128

Oriental Movie Metropolis 77

Pacino, Al 123
Palme d'Or 135
Paramount Pictures 10, 27, 28
Paul, Robert W. 96
Peterson, Bob 37
Pictures of Time Warner 28
Pixar 38-9, 100, 103
Poehler, Amy 110-1
post-production 94-5
POV shot 21
pre-production 42-3
premieres 124, 125
principal photography 74-5
Pritt, Brad 63
producer 50
production assistant 55
production companies 38-9
production design 44-5
prop maker 67
props 17, 66-7
publicity stunts 125

Rachesky, Mark 33
ratings 123
Ray, Nicholas 56
re-shoot 75
Reeves, Keanu 93
release date 122-3
RKO Radio Pictures 27, 87
Robbins, Tim 30-1
Rooftop Curtain Cinema 128
Ruttenberg, Joseph 81
Rydstrom, Gary 85

schedule 68-9
Schoonmaker, Thelma 97
Scorsese, Martin 97
Scott, Ridley 51
screenplay 17, 34-5, 36-7
Selznick, David O. 44
Serkis, Andy 88, 89
set designers 58-9
sets 17, 58-9
shot list 47
Silver Lion 134
Smith, George Albert 11
Sony Pictures Animation 12
Sony studios 12
sound design 108-9
soundstage 76-7
soundtrack 84-5

Spielberg, Steven 16-7, 72
Steiner, Max 112
storyboard 17, 46-7
Streep, Meryl 15
Studio Ghibli 13
studio 10-11, 12-13, 26-7, 28-9
stunts 90-3
subtitles 111
Sunset Bronson Studios 77
Sutherland, Ivan 104

talent agencies 15, 48
teasers 120
Thompson, Emma 34
3D films 23
title sequence 114-5
tracking shot 21
trailers 121
treatments 16
Tri Star Pictures 12
Turner, Edward 11
20th Century Fox 27, 28, 41, 119

unit production manager 53
United International 119
Universal Pictures 28, 29

Venice Film Festival 134
vertical distribution 119
visual effects 98-9, 100-1

Walt Disney Animation
    Studios 106-7
Walt Disney Pictures 28, 29, 46
Warner Bros. 10, 27, 28, 119
Watson, Emma 15
WETA Digital 39
Wiig, Kristen 50
Williams, Richard 95
Williams, Robin 64

143

PICTURE CREDITS

Picture credits
(t=top, b=bottom, l=left, r=right, c=center, fc=front cover, bc=back cover)

AllStar Picture Library: 45b LucasFilm.

Getty: 14-15c Samir Hussein, 20b Ullstein Bild, 24b Marcel Thomas, 27b Donaldson Collection, 33r Ann Cusack, 38-39c Justin Sullivan, 44-45c Selznick/MGM, 46-47c Earl Theisen Collection, 48-49c Dario Cantatore, 54-55c Keith Hampshire, 55b Spencer Weiner, 62-63c E Charbonneau, 66b Peter MacDiarmid, 106-107c Bloomberg, 114l Alfred Eisenstaedt, 118r George Rose, 120-121c Frederic J. Brown, 121r Jonathan Leibson, 124-125c Leon Neal, 124b Ernest Ruscio, 125t Jeff J Mitchell, 128b The Age, 129b Michael Buckner, 132-133c Kevin Winter, 133t Karwai Tang.

Kobal Collection 2-3 Walt Disney Pictures, 4t & 16-17c Fotos International, 4b & 61r Lionsgate, 5t & 93b Warner Bros., 5c & 105t Dreamworks, 5b & 131l Ladd Company/Warner Bros., 6-7c Universal/Wing Nut Films, 6r RKO, 7t Paramount, 11t Warner Bros./First National, 11b & 66-67 MGM, 14m Marvel Studios/Rosenthal Zade, 18-19c Regency Enterprises, 20l P.E.A, 21t DANJAQ/Eon Productions, 21b 20th Century Fox, 22-23c Paramount, 24r Amblin/Legendary Pictures/Universal, 25t Paramount, 29b Walt Disney Pictures, 30-31c Spelling Films International, 31t Touchstone, 32-33c 20th Century Fox/Paramount, 34-35c New Line/Saul Zaentz, Wing Nut, 34l Ruby Films, 36-37c Dreamworks, 37t Universal, 49b Columbia/Goldcrest 50-51c 20th Century Fox/David Appleby, 51b Paramount/Miramax, 52b Tequila Gang/Warner Bros., 56-57c New Line/Saul Zentz/Wing Nut, 58-59c 20th Century Fox/Paramount/Merie W. Wallace, 59t Warner Bros., 60-61c MGM, 61t 20th Century Fox, 63b 20th Century Fox/Blue Wolf, 64-65c Columbia/American Zoetrope/Sony, 65t Paramount/Howell Conat, 65b Lionsgate, 68-69 Warner Bros., 70-71 20th Century Fox/Genre Films/International Traders/Mid Atlantic Films/Giles Keyte, 74-75c Lucasfilm/Bad Robot Productions/Walt Disney Studios/David James, 76-77c DANJAQ/EON/UA, 78-79c Paramount, 80-81c Warner Bros., 81c Warner Bros., 81b MGM, 82b Warner Bros., 83b Hammer, 84-85c Amblin/Universal, 84b Marvel, 86-87c Warner Bros./Village Roadshow Pictures/Jason Boland, 86r Warner Bros./Village Roadshow Pictures/Jason Boland, 87t Korda, 88-89c New Line Cinema, 89t Columbia Pictures, 90-91c Bad Robot Productions/Skydance Productions/Paramount, 90b United Artists, 91t Lawrence Gordon/Mutual Film/Paramount/Alex Bailey, 92-93c Lucasfilm/Paramount, 92t Concord/Warner Bros., 92mr Europacorp/TF1 Corp, 92m 20th Century Fox/Bazmark Films, 92br StudioCanal Films, 92b Warner Bros./Village Roadshow /Wallace Merrie W., 93r DANJAQ/EON/Sony, 95b Allied Film Makers, 96-97c Zoetrope/United Artists, 97t Dreamworks, 97b Paramouht/GK Films, 98-99c Walt Disney Pictures, 98b MGM, 99t Meiles, 100-101c Walt Disney Pictures, 101r 20th CenturyFox/Genre Films/International Traders/ Mid Atlantic Films, 102-103c Dreamworks/Universal, 102l MGM, 103b Warner Bros./Village Roadshow Pictures, 104-105c Aardman/StudioCanal, 105mr Studio Ghibli, 105b 20th Century Fox, 106l Walt Disney Pictures, 107t Legendary Pictures, 107c Warner Bros., 109t Zoetrope/United Artists, 109b Lucasfilm/20th Century Fox, 110-111 Reel FX Creative Studios/Realitivity Media, 111b Columbia/Sony, 114-115 Lucasfilm/Bad Robot/Walt Disney Studios, 115t Paramount, 116-117c Illumination Entertainment/Universal Pictures, 116l, 117t Color Force/Lionsgate.

Rex Features: 25b Moviestore Collection, 112-113c Jonathan Player.

Shutterstock: 1 & 144 Suat Gursozlu, 4-5c & 144 Kostiantyn Karpenko, 8-9c Everett Collection, 8l Everett Historical, 9t Everett Historical, (Movie Facts clapperboards) Aleksandr Bryliaev, 10-11c trekandshoot, 10l neftali, 11b Anton Ivanov, 12-13c kowition, 12 Anton Ivanov, 13t nito, 13b testing, 14, 83, 93, 97, 105, 107, 113, 115 & 136-137 (Popcorn) ElkhatiebVector, 15t rivsoft, 15r s_bukley, 15b Featureflash Photo Agency, 17b Sergey Laventev, 19c Jonathan Player, 19r Stocklite, 21r sculpies, 22b Debarti CGI, 23t shippee, 23b Tyler Olsen, 24-25c Sascha Preussner, 24-25 WindVector, 26-27c Gerry Boughan, 26l Everett Historial, 27c Oscity, 28-29c Capture Light, 28b Capture Light, 29r Sarunyu L, 31b Alexander Kirch, 32b Studio DMM Photography, Designs & Art, 35t FunFunPhoto, 37b Featureflash Photo Agency, 38b Featureflash Photo Agency, 39t Featureflash Photo Agency, 40-41c Ververidis Vasilis, 41t Moso Image, 42-43c q katz, 43b littleny, 45t. Lucy Clark, 47t DFLC Prints, 48b Jaguar PS, 48b Helga Esteb, 51r s_bukley, 52-53c fabiodevilla, 53r Sean Pavone, 57t Lauren Orr, 57c UTBP, 57b Vlad G, 58b Danussa, 67t nikkytok, 69b rawpixel.com, 71b Pavel L Photo and Video, 71t J. Henning Buchholz, 72-73c Pavel L Photo and Video, 73b Legend_art, 74b Everett Collection, 75b Yulia Grigoryeva, 78b James Steidl, 79t Jgolby, 82-83c IR Stone, 88b DFree, 94-95c, 95t Eldar Nukovic, 100b s_bukley, 106-107tc Cary Westfall, 107r Joe Seer, 108-109c Mihai Simonia, 113t Featureflash Photo Agency, 113b Featureflash Photo Agency, 118-119c City of Angels, 120b Lauren Elisabeth, 122-123c rmnoa357, 122b Christian Bertrand, 123 Patryk Kosmider, 126-127c Andrew Zarivny, 126b Radu Bercan, 127t Tyler Olsen, 127b LuckyImages, 128-129c Jean-Philippe Menard, 129t Everett Collection, 130-131c Vadim Ovchinnikov, 130r Manczurov, 134-135 Featureflash Photo Agency, 134r Denis Makarenko, 135t magicinfoto, (popcorn), 136-137c Raisa Kanareva, 136c Hadrian, 138-143 Margarita Nikolskaya.